MISSILES, MASKS AND MIRACLES

CHARLES SAMUEL

D1411551

LEVIATHAN PRESS

BOOKS THAT MAKE A DIFFERENCE

Nathaniel "Sunky" Katz

Friend,
Husband,
Father

This book is dedicated in memory of
our friend Nat Katz.

***

Nat never stopped believing in
God's miracles.

***

He continues to be an inspiration to
all of us who found strength in his
courage and passion for life.

MISSILES, MASKS AND MIRACLES
The Astonishing True Account of the Invisible Shield
Protecting Israel During the Gulf War
by Charles Samuel

17 Warren Road, Suite 19
Baltimore, Maryland 21208
www.leviathanpress.com (410) 653-0300

ISBN 1-881927-08-3

Printed in the United States of America
First US edition 2000
Cover and jacket design by Lightbourne Graphics
Page layout by Fisherman Sam
Editorial services by Sharon Goldinger/PeopleSpeak
Distributed to the trade by NBN (800) 462-6420
Distributed to Judaica stores by Judaica Press (800) 972-6201

Group sales:
All books from Leviathan Press are available at bulk order
discounts for educational, promotional and fund raising
purposes. Call (410) 653-0300 or (800) 538-4284.

Jewish Literacy Foundation

This edition of Missiles, Masks and Miracles is a project of the Jewish Literacy Foundation ...

...BECAUSE JEWISH LITERACY
IS THE FOUNDATION
OF JEWISH COMMITMENT

JEWISH LITERACY FOUNDATION
17 WARREN ROAD SUITE 18
BALTIMORE, MARYLAND 21208
(410) 602-1020 (877) J-LITERACY

From the author of Missiles, Masks and Miracles

Critical acclaim for—

THE JERUSALEM CONSPIRACY
by Charles Samuel

"This superbly crafted thriller will keep you turning pages late into the night. A rare and riveting insider's view of how extremists think ... and act. I loved it."
Alan M. Dershowitz

"A gripping thriller to the very last page. If I were you, I would buy a copy before the Shin Bet (Israeli Secret Service) removes all copies from the shelves."
The Jerusalem Post

"Taut, chilling and totally plausible. The Jerusalem Conspiracy is a great read that will make you think twice."
Gary Kessler, VP movies and minis, NBC

"This book will shake you up ... Riveting from beginning to end."
Larry King

MISSILES

"A flaming chunk of missile landed in the middle of our apartment, setting everything on fire. I dialed the emergency number and yelled into the phone, 'The missile's in my living room, and it's burning down my house!' I helped my wife into the car. Then I ran back up to the apartment we had lived in for twenty-one years. But the smoke was too thick. I couldn't save anything. Thank God we're still alive." [1]

MASKS

"Everything around me was destroyed. The walls had fallen down and the ceiling had collapsed. I didn't even have time to put on my mask when everything came crashing down around me. I live on the ground floor; and above me three stories had collapsed. We were all huddled together—me, my wife and our children. The wooden clothes closet fell on my wife. She was screaming hysterically. It was terrible. Afterward it became clear that the closet had fallen at such an angle that it shielded my wife from the heavy rubble of the walls and concrete. She escaped with only five stitches in her forehead. The rest of us were unharmed." [2]

MIRACLES

"Our house was seriously damaged during the first attack. Luckily, at the time of the explosion, neither of us was at home. We couldn't take the tension, so we decided to visit some friends out of town. We got into our car and headed north. Then, on the way, we heard the siren and then the explosion. The windows of the car blew out, and a piece of missile came in through the tailgate and exited through the right-hand door, flying inches past my wife's head." [3]

Dedicated to my wife Chana,
the true hero in our family.

CONTENTS
▲▲▲▲▲▲▲▲▲▲▲▲

PROLOGUE

Waiting Until Dark   17

PART I - A STORM IN THE DESERT

Whose War Is This Anyway?   31
A War with No Warriors   35
The Strain of Restraint   39
CNN Live - From My Backyard   47

PART II - MISSILES

Scuds - The Rain of Terror   55
We're All Patriots   61
The 39 Lashes   69

PART III - MASKS

Conventional, Gas or Worse?   77
Faces Behind the Mask   83
The Russians are Coming - Still?   91
Sadly, It's a Small World Too   99
Growing Arab Support in Israel - For Saddam!   105
From Babylon to Jerusalem and Back   111

Part IV - Miracles

From Lucky to Miraculous   123
Even the Believers Can't Believe It   135
The Lawyer's Reprieve   143

Epilogue

The End is Just the Beginning   151

Notes   154
About the Author   156

Preface:

Living Through The Storm

February 1991
Purim

This book was written in 1991 while Operation Desert Storm was raging in the Persian Gulf.

I started working on this manuscript after the twenty-ninth missile fell somewhere in Israel. By the time the war had ended, a total of thirty-nine missiles had crashed down around us. The stories are true, but the names and places have been changed or altered. This was done originally for two reasons: to protect the surviving families from the onslaught of curiosity seekers and interviewers, and to conceal information from the Iraqis about the exact location and damage done by specific missile attacks. I hope they have fired their last missile, but one never knows. In the course of interviewing government officials and rescue personnel, I discovered stories that showed how closely

Israel came to suffering major disasters. Due to security restrictions, these stories cannot be told at this time.

The material for this book was drawn from eyewitness accounts and reports in the Israeli Hebrew and English press, radio and television. This book would not have been possible without the tremendous efforts made by countless reporters and photographers in the early days of the war. Because many of the stories that were circulating throughout the country were so incredible, I decided to limit the accounts in this book to those that could be confirmed by at least one additional newspaper account or by interviews with firsthand witnesses.

In the case of accounts originally told in Hebrew, I adopted a free translation instead of a literal one in order to make the accounts more readable to an English-speaking audience. I made every effort to avoid embellishing these stories: they speak for themselves.

I would like to express my gratitude to the various Israeli government ministries for providing valuable information. Special thanks are due to the Israel Government Press Office and its staff. And an understated thank you goes to the American and Israeli soldiers who manned the Patriot batteries and to the United States led forces who had the courage to confront evil and help make my home a safer place to live.

The following people should also be singled out for their assistance on this project: Rabbi Noah Weinberg, Dean of Aish HaTorah, for his encouragement, enthusiasm and support for this project. Mordechai

Haller for his research. R. Shmuel Silinsky for his research of the Biblical passages. Mrs. Carol Topf for her research and translation. Menachem Gottlieb and Robbie Berman for their original interviews. Mrs. Yonina Hall for her editing assistance. R. Chaim Dubin for his computer expertise. Ben Tripp for his help with the photographs. Ken Spiro for his advice. Henoch Kosberg for his assistance. Sharon Friedman for her encouragement and best efforts. Shimon Apisdorf and his team at Leviathan Press for believing in this project. My sister Carolynne for her help and advice. My parents and my father-in-law who have since passed away, and my mother-in-law who probably suffered more during the missile attacks than we did. And my children for always being a source of joy and blessing

My wife Chana is the true hero of the war in our family and deserves the credit for this book becoming a reality as quickly as it did. She created a warm, loving environment in our home despite the stress of missile attacks—let alone the stress of dealing with a husband writing a book. She is my constant companion and best editor and critic.

Finally, I would like to thank the One whose invisible hand protected me, my family and all the others mentioned (or not mentioned) within these pages. May He soon bring peace to Israel and all nations.

Charles Samuel
Jerusalem
Purim 5751 / February 1991

Prologue:

Waiting
Until
Dark

◀
◀
◀
◀
◀
◀
◀
◀
◀
◀
◀
◀
◀

January 23, 1991

The streets of Israel are quiet but tense.
People scurry home before nightfall.
Attacks always come under the cover of darkness.

The entire country has been under a twenty-four-hour emergency alert since the outbreak of the Gulf War. A special radio station has been designated to broadcast "silence" all night long; crackling to life only in the event of a missile attack. Soldiers on reserve duty are stationed throughout the country and listen carefully, day and night, waiting for the Hebrew code words, *Nachash Zepha*—"Poisonous Viper."

Poisonous Viper, a hauntingly appropriate choice of words, serves as the warning for the imminent impact of deadly Scud missiles.

This is what happened in our home that night:

I had been struggling to stay up late every night to catch the last details of CNN's daily news summary. The psychologists say, "The more you know, the calmer you are." I think I'm beginning to suffer from "paralysis by over-analysis." Anyway, after that particular night's broadcast, I switched off the TV and tuned the radio to the special "silent channel."

I fussed around for a few minutes until I finally found a comfortable spot on my pillow. I glanced over at my wife Chana and four-week-old son who had been sleeping and snuggling with us for the past few hours. We named the baby Shalom (Peace), after my great-grandfather. We hoped his name would be an omen for the future.

Just as I began to doze off, the radio announcer blasted out: "Nachash Zepha, Nachash Zepha!" I wish they had chosen something less terrifying than "poisonous viper" for the code words. A lump instantly formed in my throat, like it must have for thousands of other insomniacs still awake enough to hear the signal. I sat straight up in my bed. The sirens started wailing on the radio. Then I heard the muffled sound of the local siren coming through our sealed bedroom window. I knew my friend Yitzchak was on reserve guard duty in our neighborhood and that he had been the one who sounded the siren. I wondered how he was feeling, knowing that his wife and children were home alone.

I yelled out, "It's a real attack Chana, Let's get going!" I felt bad about having to wake her up. She's been so tired lately with all the children out of school and at home for the past few weeks. She sort of grunted out of her sleep and then jumped to action. Even though it was dark, I sensed the panic on her face. We really had to hurry to get everything and everybody ready in time. You only have two minutes from the time the siren sounds until a Scud, or a huge piece of one blasted by a defending Patriot missile, comes crashing down somewhere at random in Israel.

Before the war, army experts assured civilians that there would be at least a four-hour warning period before any Scud missile attack could be expected from western Iraq. The actual flight time of the missiles is seven minutes, but Allied satellites were supposed to be able to observe the beginning of the time-consuming set-up and fueling process. Now the Iraqis are preparing the missiles unnoticed. All that remains for a warning is seven minutes. Five of these minutes are required to transmit the satellite signal; first to the United States for processing and then back to the Israeli military. Only two minutes are left for civilians to react and do whatever they need to do. Because the threat of a poisonous gas attack exists, the army has requested that each family select one room in a house to be hermetically sealed in the event of an air raid. This is recommended even though it exposes the population to a greater risk if the enemy uses conventional warheads. A dilemma with the most deadly of potential consequences.

These gas-proof rooms are sealed by taping heavy-gauge plastic around windows and sealing doors by applying brown plastic tape around the frames. In the event of an attack, you seal yourself and your family inside—and you wait and pray.

The door to a gas-proof room is sealed with heavy duty plastic and tape.

Atwo-minute warning in the early evening was bad enough, but now with everyone sound asleep and the lights out, it was really going to be a mad dash through the apartment. Chana rushed to the girls' room and shook Esther Leah, our six year old. Somehow she coaxed her to walk to our bedroom without stopping at the bathroom. Sadly, the routine has become all too familiar. I ran to the boys' room and scooped up Eli, our three year old. He made some jerking motions as I picked him up, but as usual he stayed asleep. I dropped him on our bed.

Ninety seconds left.

I headed for the girls' room to grab our four year old, Rachel. Chana sidestepped the toys on her way to take Yonah out of his crib. Holding Rachel in my arms, I bumped into Chana and Yonah as they turned the corner in the hallway. I let them go first. Dashing into our room, I slammed the door behind us.

Only one minute left, but at least we were all together in our sealed room.

I yanked two gas masks out of the cupboard and tossed one to Chana. We released the black rubber straps and stretched the headpieces over our heads. If you didn't do it just right, it would pinch your hair. I forgot to take off my glasses and had to start again, losing a few precious seconds. As I adjusted the mask on my face, I felt like a player suiting up for the big game, but this was no game—this was the real thing.

Forty-five seconds left.

Chana's job was to help the kids with their masks. She started with the girls because they're old enough to put them on themselves—in theory. Esther Leah, our six year old, decided she needed to go to the bathroom first. Rachel complained that she was too tired to put her mask on. Chana pulled the plastic bag containing dirty diapers out of the diaper pail, and presto chango, instant potty! Esther Leah was happy, but Rachel still refused to budge.

Thirty seconds left; still no masks on the kids.

Through the pandemonium I thought I heard a dull thud. Was it a Scud landing? A Patriot? It could have even been one of the neighbor's kids upstairs dropping his gas mask on the floor. I wasn't sure.

My job was to close the door and seal it with the brown plastic tape while the kids were putting on their masks. There was still plenty of tape on the door frame from previous attacks, but some gaps needed to be fixed. I scraped my fingernail around the roll four times; finally, I found the edge. With a quick snap, I tore back a two-foot strip of tape. The screech of the tape separating from the roll woke up the baby and he started to cry.

It's amazing to think that exactly fifty years ago, my father, his sister, four brothers and my grandparents were hiding in a bedroom about this size on the outskirts of Amsterdam. Then, the madman was from Berlin, not Baghdad. They hid there for almost three years from the Nazis—most of the time, in that one tiny room. They also had a bucket for a toilet. Their alarm wasn't a siren, but the panicky voice of the teenage daughter of the family in whose home they were hiding. She would yell out, "The Nazis are coming! They're raiding the houses searching for Jewish people. Quick!" And the whole family would have two minutes to scramble into a secret hiding place behind a false panel in the cupboard.

There was a triangular crawl space under a staircase that all eight of them had to squeeze into. The Nazi soldiers entered the room and began banging on the walls and floorboards listening for the hollow echo of a hiding place. The banging came within inches of their faces. They held their breath. On the inside of the false panel my grandfather had hung a blanket, that muffled the sound. Miraculously, the Germans left, and in a few minutes they could come out of their stuffy hiding place. Unlike Anne Frank, they all survived the war.

My whole life I heard stories like that about the war, but I couldn't relate to them. Now it was happening to me. For the first time, I was beginning to understand the feeling of helplessness, the fear for the safety of my wife and children, the irrational hatred and persecution of Jews, and the need to hope for a miracle.

My thoughts were interrupted by a voice on the radio: "This is a real attack. All citizens are requested to immediately put on your gas masks and go to your sealed rooms."

I turned around and Chana had already pushed the two babies through the small openings in their plastic *gas-proof tents. Eli refused to put on his mask and the girls were still fiddling with theirs. Chana shrugged her shoulders.*

Three minutes passed. We missed the deadline.

We didn't know if we should expect an explosion or gas. Should we force the masks on the girls? Just at that moment, the announcer broke in and said not to force the masks on the children because the sealed room provided adequate protection. We decided to break the tension by singing along with the kids to the songs being broadcast in between radio announcements. Things were so hectic in the room that we didn't have time to think about the missiles on their way to Israel.

The Israeli Army appointed Brigadier General Nachman Shai as the official radio spokesman for the duration of the war. His job is to keep the civilian population calm during a missile attack and to give them instructions about when they could remove their masks and leave their sealed rooms. To help minimize confusion and to allow the army to release segments of the population as quickly as possible, the country has been divided into six sections, each represented by a different letter of the Hebrew alphabet.

That's when Nachman Shai came over the radio. Everybody loves him. If he ran for prime minister, he'd probably win. In his easygoing, raspy voice, that seems to calm everyone down, he said, "Again there has been a missile launched from western Iraq. It has already landed. Those of you in areas Aleph (A), Bet (B), Gimmel (C), Dalet (D), and Vav (F) can remove your masks, have a drink of water and leave your sealed rooms. I'd like to ask residents of area Heh(E) to remain in their sealed rooms, and keep their masks on until we can determine the exact location—and if the warhead was conventional or chemical."

As soon as we heard the letter Aleph (A), we tore our masks off. It gets very hot inside of them very quickly and you sweat a lot where the rubber touches your skin. We collected the kids and took them back to their rooms. The whole incident took twenty minutes from the time the siren first sounds until the children were back in bed.

As soon as the kids were settled, Chana climbed back under the covers. She said she had to get some sleep—not as a complaint but simply as a fact. She asked me if I was going back to sleep. I was still really wound-up and told her I couldn't fall asleep until I found out if anyone was hurt. The territories hadn't yet received the all clear.

I stared up at the ceiling. I felt as if my insides had been put through a food processor. I was relieved that we made it safely through another attack, but I was concerned about how Chana was coping. I was proud of how well the kids were taking things and yet not hiding their own fears. I was apprehensive about another attack. But most of all, at that moment, I was worried about who might have been hurt from the attack that just occurred.

> A *few minutes later, Nachman Shai reported that a single Scud had fallen. There were no reported injuries. Some damage was done to a few buildings. "Another miracle," I thought to myself.*
>
> *I glanced over at my wife who was trying to get a few hours of sleep before the baby woke up to nurse— hoping there wouldn't be another Scud attack that night. That's when I realized that she, and others like her, are the ones who are actually carrying the burden of this war.*[4]

Those on the home front were the true heroes this time. In Israel, the front lines of war have never been very far from the front steps of many soldiers' homes. Ever since the War of Independence, the Israeli home has been a sanctuary for the war-weary soldier: A calm place to regroup after facing a barrage of enemy fire. This time, that sanctuary had been brutally shattered by a madman in Iraq. Our homes became the battle-field and our comrades in arms were our wives and children.

The sanctity of the home and family was violated. Parents and children live under the constant threat of a deadly poisonous-gas attack—terrorism in its extreme. A whole country is being held hostage by fear and yet being forced to function because there is nowhere to run. The only comfort has become the realization that as the bombs continue to fall, causing enormous material damage to buildings and possessions, the people keep walking away virtually unhurt. It seems as

if the people of Israel are being protected by an
invisible shield.

The truly unbelievable tales of survival continue to
pour in from all over the country: Stories of babies
surviving unharmed in their plastic tents after walls
collapsed all around them and of families being saved
by huddling in a room designed to protect them only
from gas, while the rest of their home was destroyed by
a conventional missile. One person stayed in the
sealed room, and the living room was destroyed;
another was in his living room and the sealed room was
obliterated. One went to the bomb shelter, and the
apartment building above took a direct hit. Another
stayed in their apartment building, and the bomb
shelter beneath it was destroyed.

This book is being written as the missiles continue
to fall. It is a testimony to the heroes who survived the
attacks and lived to share, with the world, the miracles
that saved them.

*Another night of missiles brings rescue workers
to the scene hoping to find survivors.*

PART I

A
Storm
In
The
Desert

Whose War Is This Anyway?

◄ *January 19, 1991*

Iraq sits atop the second largest oil reserves in the world.

Only the royal family of Saudi Arabia controls more oil than Saddam Hussein.

In 1968 a revolution in Iraq brought Saddam Hussein to power. Since then his lust for money, prestige and honor has been insatiable.

Saddam Hussein saw himself as a modern-day Nebuchadnezzar, the mighty ruler of the ancient Babylonian empire. He wanted to succeed where Egypt's president Nasser had failed; he wanted to become the leader of a vast and unified Pan-Arab nation. To execute his plan, Saddam Hussein would have to build a formidable army. He would also have to deal with Israel, a bothersome obstacle to this grand Pan-Arab vision. All the previous wars against Israel (in 1948, 1956, 1967 and 1973) had been dismal military failures for the Arabs.

Over the years, Saddam plowed over one hundred billion dollars worth of oil profits into building the fourth largest army in the world. An additional forty billion dollars in aid from friendly oil-rich neighbors like Kuwait, Saudi Arabia and Qatar helped him construct deadly poisonous gas and biological weapons facilities. Saddam's attack on the Khomeini regime led to eight bloody years of the Iran-Iraq War.

When the war with Iran failed, Saddam looked southeast to his next neighbor, Kuwait. Ironically, Kuwait had helped Saddam purchase the weapons that were about to be used against her. On August 2, 1990, ostensibly as the result of an oil dispute, Saddam invaded Kuwait. Saddam cynically assumed that the world would stand by and that no one would come to the aid of this tiny Arab emirate.

He was wrong. The United States quickly led a United Nations campaign to condemn Saddam and impose trade sanctions. An international coalition was formed to force Iraq out of Kuwait if Saddam didn't withdraw by January 15, 1991. President George Bush drew his "line in the sand," and when the deadline passed, he gave the US led coalition forces the go ahead to launch the war.

Desert Storm, the war in the Persian Gulf, was not Israel's war. Israel was not guilty of invading Kuwait in the middle of the night. Israel was not guilty of the "Rape of Kuwait." Israel did not persuade George Bush to organize a multi-national coalition and lead the mission to liberate Kuwait. Israel was not guilty of bombing Baghdad, Kuwait, or even the missile launch sites employed against her in western Iraq. Yet somehow, this innocent bystander became the target of Saddam Hussein's missiles. The "Desert Storm" exploded over the skies of Tel Aviv as Saddam launched one deadly Scud missile after another at Israel's key population centers. It didn't make sense. But whoever said the Middle East makes sense?

Here is another story I heard first hand.

Michael is an accountant from Chicago. During a busy lunch hour on a downtown American street, probably no one would be able to pick him out in a crowd. Ten years ago he moved to Israel with his family. Usually he is at his desk in his office. Today he was sitting in a jeep patrolling the Jordanian border.

This is what Michael told me.

This whole thing is like a bad dream. Like a nightmare. I feel like my hands have been tied behind my back and I've been pushed into a boxing ring that I don't want to be in. Every time my opponent lands a punch to my face, the referee looks at the blood streaming out of my nose and says, "Hmmm, not too bad. Keep fighting. "Keep fighting?! I wish I could. It's outrageous that young American men and women are putting their lives in danger to protect us. If it's right for them to be there, we should be there with them.

So you know what our response is? The Israeli Army pulls me out of my office and takes me away from my wife and kids who are having a hard enough time as it is. And you know where they put me for a month? I have to patrol the Jordanian border with these other four *guys on this jeep. King Hussein of Jordan says this isn't his war either. His skies are sacred, "If anyone violates Jordanian air space it will be considered an act of war." I'm sure he really means it. The Scuds fly from east to west over his head, but God forbid if an Israeli jet flies high over Jordan to take out a missile before it is launched from Iraq.*

That's the most insane thing about this whole situation. Sadly, we've got the most experience in the world for taking out these kinds of targets. We bombed the nuclear reactor in Iraq in 1987. Our commandos traveled thousands of miles to rescue our hostages held at Entebbe airport. Now we have to sit here and watch the skies for incoming death.

You know what this is like? It's like you are taken hostage by terrorists in your own home. The police have the house surrounded, but the police commissioner won't call in the S.W.A.T. team because he's afraid your neighbors might complain about the noise. Can you imagine it? We've got the experience to help wipe out Saddam Hussein's terrorism, and the Arabs in the coalition won't let us help America get the job done. Our Arab neighbors hate the Jews more than they care about saving their own lives.

I can't sleep because I can't stop thinking how absurd this situation is. I can't stop worrying about my family. There's no phone out here to call them and calm them down after an attack and tell them, "Daddy will be home soon." I hope I really will be home soon.[5]

A War With No Warriors

January 19, 1991

Israel has a population of about four million people while being surrounded by one hundred million Arabs in hostile dictatorships. For this reason, virtually every adult male in Israel is required to spend one month each year in the Israel Defense Force (IDF) reserves.

During wars, in the forty-three years since the State of Israel was established, it was the fathers and husbands who went off to fight. When the wars broke out, the boys doing their three-year, post-high school tour of duty would hold the front lines until the bulk of the army—consisting of teachers, shopkeepers, laborers, professionals and businessmen—could be called up. In the midst of battle, they would return home for a rest with amazing tales of bravery and heroism, hiding the ugly realities of war from their wives and children.

In this war, however, the soldiers have no tales of bravery to tell. Some are involved in an electronic war of keyboards and computer screens surveying the skies. Others have nothing to do except patrol the empty streets of Arab villages under curfew.

This is one soldier's story:

For the past three years, the Gaza Strip has been the most dangerous place to do your reserve duty. Now, sitting in a jeep on an empty street in this refugee camp, I worry more about my wife than she worries about me. Last night we saw the incoming Scud streaking across the sky to the north. All I could think about was my children, huddled in that little room with a piece of plastic to protect them, stuffed into those frightening tents.

Iraq has its soldiers fighting on the front lines and civilians on the home front under bombardment. The Americans have a front line, but its civilians are watching the war at home on the TV. Israel has a home front that is under attack by missiles, but there are no Israeli warriors on the front line.

A surrealistic, symbiotic relationship has developed between us and the Americans. They have become our warriors, and we have become their civilians under attack. CNN has helped cement this relationship. With every siren that goes off in Tel Aviv or Jerusalem, the Americans watching on TV jump as if it is New York or

Los Angeles under attack. I hope they worry about us just as much after the war is over.[6]

This is the first war that Israel has fought in which the people at the front line, instead of preparing their military positions for attack, are in hardware stores buying sheets of plastic and brown tape to seal their bedrooms. Instead of analyzing maps of the enemy territory, they are surveying their apartments, trying to decide which room is best to hide in.

Then came an emergency call-up for some of the reserves in Israel. Extra people were needed to distribute gas masks, sound the sirens, staff emergency medical stations and clear away the rubble from neighborhoods devastated by Scud attacks.

One soldier returned home with this amazing story to tell his family:

I'm a teacher, and I received an emergency call-up for reserve duty at a hospital in the south. It was at the height of the missile attacks, and all of us were separated from our families for a month. The commander set up a rotation system for a forty-eight-hour leave on each of the three successive weekends that we would be on duty. This meant that everyone would get one Sabbath off during the month to be with his family. Fifteen men left the first weekend and returned to base. When it came time for the second group to leave, *for some inexplicable reason, the commander singled out two from the first group to have a second weekend off — meaning two soldiers would not have a weekend off that month.*

Before anyone realized the error, the soldiers and the commander had left the base. There was an uproar among the remaining thirty soldiers. Most of them lived in the Tel Aviv area and worried that they would miss out on being with their families at least one weekend that month. Fridays and Saturdays were "peak" Scud attack days.

Every one of them calmed down when they heard about the phone calls the commander received Sunday morning. Both soldiers on leave had been with their families when Scud missiles hit their houses. They lived within a mile of each other; no one in either family was injured. Even though most of the other men in our unit were also from the Tel Aviv area, none of their homes were affected. When the commander returned to the base, he told us that he didn't know why, but something made him single out those two soldiers.[7]

The Strain Of Restraint

◀ **January 20, 1991**

◀ The whole world praised Israel for her "policy of restraint."
   In the face of wave after wave of Scud missile attacks, Israel did nothing to defend herself.

Imagine Brooklyn and New Rochelle being bombed nightly and President Bush pursuing a policy of restraint. Washington well understands the problems and enormous pressures facing Israeli Prime Minister Shamir and is afraid that a rising casualty toll will make it impossible for Israel to keep its forces out of the war. The United States cannot depend on miracles every night.

Everyone expects devastation similar to what occurred in Iran when it was bombed with missiles during the Iran-Iraq war. In Teheran, each missile claimed an average of eight to ten lives and left many more wounded.

Missile barrages launched nightly at Israeli cities make the nights nerve-racking. The nation's morale is slowly eroding. In spite of the horrifying scenes of destruction, the Scuds are creating more psychological damage than physical. Israelis are called *Sabras*, the Hebrew word for the the fruit of the cactus: Prickly on the outside and soft on the inside. This war had turned the *Sabras* inside out. Everybody is putting up a calm exterior, yet their insides are being jabbed with constant pangs of fear. Every Israeli is stricken with the feeling of, "It could happen to us."

I recall another story reported in the press:

The area has been sealed off by the police. People are wandering around aimlessly, in complete silence. They walk slowly. They are bewildered. Just yesterday this was a street alive with the happy squeals of playing children: Now it's a war zone. It is hard to digest the terrible sight.

The residents look at the remains of what were once their homes and don't know where to begin. Rescue workers take time off from their demolition work to help people find some of the possessions that matter most— photo albums, a child's doll, a pair of candlesticks that belonged to someone's grandmother. The searching is done delicately, steering clear of the shattered glass and jagged pieces of broken concrete.

In a house hit directly by a Scud, only a few cracked walls are left. The whole front of the building has been torn away. The top of the main staircase is cut off and reaches into the open sky. Standing silently in an open *room is a small girl. A rescue worker yells up to her, telling her to come down before the whole building collapses. She seems to be in a trance and doesn't answer. He shouts at her again, and this time she wakes up from her dream. She quietly tells him that she is only looking for her slippers, but she can't find them.*[8]

Yet the Israeli public is learning to live with "the missile war." There is widespread understanding of the policy of restraint, and people are trying as much as possible to get back to normal, in spite of the constant strain.

Mothers are affected more than most.

We *can't take this much longer. I'm not talking about the missiles—only a few tiles from our roof went flying and some windows broke. All of that can be fixed. It's the constant tension that is getting to us. Take last night. We were getting ready to have supper when I sent my eighteen-year-old daughter to pick up my father from his apartment nearby. A few minutes after she left, the siren went off. I thought I was going to go out of my mind with worry. Those were horrible moments. The missile exploded right in our neighborhood, and all I could do was wait for my daughter to return safely with my father. Today I've started to calm down, but I still get chills when I think that the missile missed my house by only a few yards.*[9]

Television is one way to escape from the reality of war. From the first night of the conflict, Israeli television began broadcasting twenty-four hours a day. Extra programming consisting of light entertainment and comedy shows are aired to help people forget about their worries. But in one case, this backfired.

L ast Thursday night we were watching "The Cosby Show." I was taping it at the same time for a friend. Just then, the siren sounded. We dropped everything and hurried to our sealed room. After the all-clear was sounded, I realized we had left the video tape recorder on. Thinking that it would help everyone calm down, I rewound the tape so we could watch the show from the beginning.

The whole family sat down again to watch. Suddenly, the word "Alarm" appeared on the screen, signaling that a missile attack was in progress. We all rushed back to the sealed room. We put on our gas masks, and I turned on the radio but the usual emergency messages weren't being broadcast. That's when I realized that the alarm on the TV had been videotaped earlier from the real attack. That experience really shook us up.[10]

Hotlines have been established to offer advice on how to cope. Psychologists man the phones on radio call-in shows. Even a special children's television program called This Too Will Pass, is broadcast live. Not only does it give some mothers a welcome break from the stress of having children home all day, but it is also a way to help the kids cope with their feelings. Children are encouraged to draw pictures of Saddam Hussein, Scud missiles, Patriots or other images of the war and fax them directly to the host of the show who is live on camera.

The stress on the children and the potential impact it could have on them as adults are what worries people the most.

This story was told by a child who heard the code word "poisonous viper," that is broadcast on the radio seconds before the sirens go off.

When we heard the terrifying cry of "Nachash Zepha, Nachash Zepha!" we all ran to the sealed room. We were surprised when we turned on the radio and didn't hear the usual emergency instructions. We took off our masks and looked at each other. Then I heard my pet parrot scream out "Sharav Kaved" (which means "heat wave," the radio signal for "all clear") from the dining room. Apparently my parrot had learned to imitate the radio code words.[11]

Many of the older citizens in Israel are survivors of the Nazi Holocaust. The threat of extermination by poison gas that had been supplied by Germany to Iraq brings back memories they've spent a lifetime trying to forget. Each air-raid siren causes them to relive their suffering. Others, veterans of the perilous early days of

Israel, remember the horrors of Arab attacks against Jews. When the siren sounds and forces them into their sealed rooms, again they are overcome with the fear of extermination, as described below.

As soon as I heard the first siren, I ran to my grandparents' house nearby. I could still hear the alarm coming from the direction of the area behind the market when there was a loud explosion, and a brilliant flash of lightning lit up the sky. The unbelievable had happened. A missile fell on Tel Aviv. On the quiet street, I repeated the words out loud, "A missile fell on Tel Aviv." I ran to my grandfather's house. He didn't hear the alarm. Neither had my grandmother.

When as a child I was sick, my grandfather would come to my bed, gently wake me up, and feed me, dress me or read me a story. Now, thirty years later, I came to his bed to gently awaken a ninety-year-old child. His legs no longer responded to his wishes, and I would support him as he hastened to the sealed room. I would also help him with his gas mask, because his arms no longer supported him either.

I sat with him in the sealed kitchen and my grandmother sat at his side. I also put a mask on her. There we were in the room, wearing masks, three people disguised as elephants. My grandfather trembled. A ninety year-old man.

During the War of Independence, the Arabs from Jaffa would fire directly into the room in which we were *now sitting. My grandfather would wake my mother and hurry her and the rest of the family into the kitchen, where a brick wall had been built to act as a barrier against the bullets. Forty-three years have passed since then, but nothing has changed. Instead of a brick wall, we sealed the room with plastic. Instead of bullets, missiles are falling. And behold, he is already ninety years old. In any other place in the world, a man of ninety is already free of such things—good and bad— and can play away his remaining years in peace; only in Israel does nothing change. Three generations of my family hiding in the same room; building protective walls, wearing masks, and nothing changes.*[12]

CNN: Live From My Backyard

January 21, 1991

The Gulf War is the first war in history being fought "live" on television.

Even though the Vietnam War had more film coverage from the front lines and was eventually dubbed "The Living Room War," there is something eerie about watching this war as it unfolds. A network of highly sophisticated communications satellites broadcasts images of the Gulf War simultaneously to hundreds of millions of viewers around the world. As a result, viewers actually become participants in the conflict.

One civilian with relatives in America relates to the situation like this:

The strangest thing in this strange war are the moments after the missiles land. You want to know exactly where it happened, and you don't have the patience to wait for the vague announcements of the army spokesman and the telephone rumors that come in bit by bit during the day. So you call your relatives in America who are sitting in front of their television sets watching CNN. They can tell us almost immediately— from across the ocean—precisely where the missile landed, right down to the nearest intersection. They know from television reports that we are all right. They have calmed down even before we have. What a strange war.[13]

Thanks to modern communication, families separated by continents can be brought together to face the crisis.

E *very time the siren goes off, the phone rings. It is my mother in Washington D.C. She is tuned in to CNN's live coverage and is calling to make sure her adult children in Jerusalem are gathered in their sealed rooms and wearing their gas masks. On one occasion, when the siren in Tel Aviv went off before the one in Jerusalem, so did the phone.*

"The siren went off," she insisted despite our denials, "and it will sound in Jerusalem any minute, too." Sure enough, it did. She told us what the American networks were broadcasting. It created the feeling that we were going through it all together.

Then, when the all-clear siren went off, she called again to see that we removed our masks and, even from such a distance, shuffled us all back to bed.[14]

Another person with family in the United States was able to find a silver lining in this very dark cloud.

I slept through the first sirens because they weren't loud enough. What did wake me up on several occasions, however, were calls from my family in the United States. Even my ex-wife called to tell me to put on my mask, as Israeli alerts were instantly reported over CNN. This is the first time I have not resented my ex-wife telling me what to do.[15]

The Israeli Army restricts information about the location and damage of the Scud attacks. This information, if released, could help Saddam adjust his aim with future missiles, so now there is confusion about exactly what is happening during each attack.

One son, living in relatively safe Jerusalem, worried about his father back in America.

When the siren goes off, it takes us about five minutes to gather everyone into the sealed room and put the gas masks on. In the hustle and bustle, we're too preoccupied to worry. When things finally settle down in the room and we have a chance to *think about what is happening, seven minutes have passed. If we haven't heard an explosion by then, we can relax, because the missile has already landed somewhere else.*

In the meantime, my poor father who has a heart condition is glued to his television set six thousand miles away. CNN reports live from Tel Aviv that the sirens are wailing, indicating incoming Scuds. Then they pass the broadcast back to Atlanta for a five minute comment from some military analyst. Then a commercial. Then an update from Saudi Arabia. Twenty minutes later, they return to Tel Aviv, where the reporter tells Atlanta that a Scud has landed, but Israel military authorities will not allow them to divulge where it struck. It can take another ten minutes before they find out that Jerusalem wasn't affected. It's amazing—the whole world is hearing "live" all the news that "isn't" happening twenty-four hours a day!

I finally called my father and begged him to watch only five minutes of news every hour. The stress is too much for him. Even here, Israel radio plays music between announcements while we are waiting in our sealed rooms.[16]

One beneficiary of the live coverage of the war and the sirens going off in Israel has been the Israel Telephone Company. After one weekend attack, it registered 750,000 calls placed between the United

States and Israel in one hour alone—compared to the usual hourly total of 3,000 calls.

Phone calls weren't just being placed to America. A special fund was set up to allow Ethiopian immigrants to call their relatives free of charge. Although the war is receiving daily coverage in Addis Ababa, most callers are shocked to discover that the reporting isn't the CNN version.

One immigrant related his story this way:

Until a month ago, I would call to find out that everything was all right over there in Ethiopia. Now the roles are reversed. When I called after Saturday night's attack, they wouldn't believe me when I told them I was safe and sound. Their radio reported that the attack had destroyed an Israeli city and that thousands of people had been killed in Scud attacks. I've heard other cases of people calling relatives who are waiting to immigrate to Israel and being told that they had heard rumors that eleven thousand homes were destroyed and four Israeli towns were completely demolished. It seems the rumors are being spread by radio stations controlled by Iraqi-supported Eritrean rebels who are fighting against President Mengistu.[17]

Notwithstanding all the tension that live coverage has created, it has also generated comical moments as reporters try to "outscoop" each other with ever more dazzling eyewitness reports. One reporter tantalizingly waved his gas mask and glanced over his shoulder during a Scud attack in Riyadh. Israel Deputy Foreign Minister Binyamin Netanyahu donned his mask during a live interview in Tel Aviv. An Israeli radio reporter wanting to record the sound of a Scud missile exploding leaned out of his window, holding on to a microphone. After the blast, he was left holding the wire—the microphone had flown out of his hand!

A local comedian had this to say about the reporting.

CNN *has been amazing with its coverage. I wouldn't be surprised if Peter Arnett rode a Scud as it flew from Iraq to Israel just to get the story. "We're crossing Jordan now," he would say. "I see Tel Aviv in the distance."*[18]

PART II

Missiles

Scuds: The Rain Of Terror

January 22, 1991

In the history of modern warfare, the most devastating damage to civilian population centers has been done by aerial bombardment.

Cities in Europe were leveled during World War II. Dresden and Rotterdam had to be completely rebuilt. Thousands of innocent victims were killed by German bombers and V1 and V2 rockets launched against British cities. Now it is Tel Aviv's turn—although this isn't the first time the city had been attacked from the air.

In September 1939, at the beginning of World War II, the Italian Air Force bombed residential neighborhoods in the Israeli coastal city. A total of one hundred seventeen people were killed and three hundred sixty-six were wounded. Later in the war, in June 1941, enemy planes again attacked Tel Aviv and killed twelve people.

During the Israeli War of Independence, the Egyptian air force struck Tel Aviv three times in May and June of 1948. More than fifty people were killed, and many more were wounded.

The toll of one hundred and eighty dead and four hundred and forty wounded resulted from conventional bombs of World War II vintage. Now, with Israel under the threat of Scuds, the stakes are much higher. This time, a two hundred and fifty-kilogram bomb is mounted on a missile traveling at nine times the speed of sound. The shock wave alone can knock down buildings and kill hundreds of civilians trapped inside. Even without a warhead, the heat and vibration caused by a Scud's impact can cause devastating fire and damage. The Scud missile leaves a huge crater upon impact, and buildings are crushed in its wake.

Saddam Hussein acquired the deadly Scud missile from the Russians during the height of the Cold War. The Soviets had developed them with the assistance of German scientists who were captured at the end of World War II. The Scud is an outgrowth of the German V2 rocket that was successfully launched against England during World War II.

Basically, the Scud is a liquid-fueled, single-stage rocket carrying a high explosive charge in its warhead. It must be aimed very accurately, taking weather into account, because once the Scud is launched, its flight path cannot be altered.

When the Iraqis acquired these missiles, they had to adapt them because their original specifications would not allow them to reach Iraq's principal target—Israel.

Western experts helped Saddam upgrade the distance these missiles could travel. This was achieved by two methods: decreasing the weight of the warhead to a five hundred-pound payload (the Iraqis called this model the "Al Hussein") or increasing the missile's range by welding an extra four-foot section onto the end (this model was dubbed the "Al Abbas").

Knowing that Saddam's targets were to be civilian population centers, Israeli Civil Defense authorities anticipated thousands of casualties. It's no wonder that after thirty-nine Scud attacks, people couldn't believe that only one death was directly attributed to the missiles. (The other twelve deaths were primarily elderly people who suffered heart attacks due to fear, or because of improper use of their gas masks.)

The damage from a Scud is not only physical, it's also emotional. The missiles destroy far more than just buildings and property; they destroy homes and possessions that have a lifetime of memories attached to them.

This is but one personal story:

The destruction was horrifying. The whole area looked like a battlefield. Everything was scorched and uprooted. Cars were burnt out. People wandered around with bits and pieces of broken belongings, the remains of what was once furniture. Two people were struggling to dig out a personal treasure.

There is no lament, only a sobering effect on everyone and a sense of looking inward. An elderly woman found an old photograph of her son. Another dragged a vacuum cleaner towards a large shipping container with his last name written on it. There were two rows of containers, one for each family. One salvaged a refrigerator; another, a living room cabinet. A third found his armchair. On the ground were shattered vases and smashed television sets.[19]

When the Israeli authorities prepared emergency medical facilities, they outfitted hospitals to absorb up to six thousand casualties in a single attack. These estimates were based on the results of Scud attacks on Teheran during the Iran-Iraq war. Many Jews who lived in Teheran at the time managed to flee and resettle in Israel. Now, Saddam's missiles were following them to Tel Aviv.

One man related his story:

I'm originally from Iran where I lived under the regime of Khomeini. In fact, I'm a graduate of Scud attacks in Teheran. One particular evening, I went up to the fourth floor in order to help an invalid who lives there. I fed him and cleaned up the dishes afterwards. As I was leaving his apartment I heard the siren and immediately after, the explosion. I don't know how, but to my surprise, I found myself on the first floor between some blocks of concrete.

After the noise subsided, I peeked into my blown-open apartment and discovered that my sealed room was totally destroyed. If I would have been in that sealed room at the time of the blast, I wouldn't be alive.

I said jokingly to my neighbor who also survived, and who is originally from Baghdad, that it looks like Saddam Hussein still wants to kill Iranians, no matter where they are. The destruction in the Ramat Gan neighborhood reminded me of the scenes of destruction in Teheran. There, the Scud missiles were much more deadly. Every Scud attack ended with tens of people killed and many more seriously wounded. People arrived at the hospitals with limbs torn off. Nurses and doctors suffered because of the injuries they had to witness and treat.

The horror of the missiles was really what brought an end to that war that dragged on for eight years. Teheran turned into a ghost town, but Khomeini's people passed a law that any person who didn't go to work would be immediately fired without severance pay and would be publicly declared an enemy of the people. People were forced into the streets without gas masks. Fear was in their eyes. The government didn't worry about appropriate protective gear for the population and didn't compensate the victims for any damage at all. Anyone who lost his home had to take care of himself by begging for mercy. The economy was in a shambles. Children were out of school. Whole streets were wiped out.

When you compare the human and material loss and the psychological damage that was done in Teheran to what has happened in Ramat Gan, it makes it easier to see the hand of Providence. Both in Tel Aviv and Ramat Gan, in spite of the great destruction, the injuries in human terms were minuscule.[20]

Zvi, a journalist, summed up the damage inflicted on his neighborhood during the first Scud attack that scored a direct hit.

Т*he sight was horrifying. "Miracle" is too small a word to describe the fine line between the bloody massacre that might have taken place here, and the small numbers of lightly wounded that actually occurred.*[21]

When asked to comment on the damage caused by the Scud missiles, Minister of Defense Moshe Arens had this to say:

W*e see sights of destruction in Israel that have not been seen in Western countries since World War II.*[22]

We're All Patriots

◄ *January 23, 1991*

Israel was ready to send its Air Force into Iraq to eliminate the threat of Scud missiles while they were still on the ground; but its hands were tied.

At the beginning of the war, Israel realized that it would be unable to send its own air force into Iraq to eliminate the Scud missile launchers on the ground. The US-led coalition was fragile, and there was a danger of the Arab allies pulling out if Israel directly entered the conflict. The Arabs could fight Saddam, but not with Jews at their side.

The only recourse to self defense was an anti-missile missile. The Israeli-developed Arrow anti-ballistic missile project was still five years down the road. The only on-the-shelf solution to the problem was the Patriot anti-aircraft missile manufactured by the Raytheon Corporation of Massachusetts.

The Patriot was originally developed as a deterrent to enemy bombers. In the mid-eighties, Raytheon engineers upgraded the Patriot so it could intercept slow- moving Scud missiles launched by the Soviet Union at European cities. The ability of the Patriot to take down missiles was limited, so Israel hoped that time would be on its side and the Arrow, a missile specifically designed to intercept computer-guided modern missiles, would be ready to combat the Iraqi threat.

On the drawing board, the Arrow has the ability to cover a much larger area than the Patriot. It can protect a large expanse of territory, not just a single city or military installation. And unlike the Patriot, the Arrow could be counted on to destroy a chemical or biological warhead at a high enough altitude to eliminate any threat to the civilian population.

The Patriot, on the other hand, could be counted on to hit its incoming target, especially when Patriots were fired in volleys of two or four. But it couldn't be counted on to kill the warhead, even if it made contact with the incoming Scud. Sometimes it would break the Scud into smaller, yet still lethal pieces.

One eyewitness shared this story:

Huge missile shards fell on the houses, smashed into roofs and split walls. When you saw the frightening lumps of metal and torn walls, you stood amazed before the enormity of the miracle. True, there was fear, there was even terror, but not one person's life *was lost in the attack. It's as if a hidden hand pushed the evil missiles away from the sealed rooms where mothers and children sat, leaving the blackened lumps of metal for souvenir hunters.*[23]

"When you saw the lumps of metal and torn walls, you stood amazed before the enormity of the miracle."

Nisim and Aviva were among the lucky ones.

A *flaming chunk of missile landed in the middle of our apartment, setting everything on fire. I dialed the emergency number and yelled into the phone, "The missile's in my living room and it's burning down my house!" I helped my wife into the car. Then I ran back up to our apartment on the third floor where we had lived for twenty-one years. But the smoke was too thick. I couldn't save anything. Thank God we're still alive.*[24]

The Patriot is a highly sophisticated and automated missile. It is just over seventeen feet long and weighs more than a ton. It has a range of more than fifty miles and travels at three times the speed of sound. its head contains conventional high explosives that blow up the intercepted target on contact.

The Patriot is more than just a missile; it is a system that contains a number of high-tech elements. Technicians sit in a mobile "Engagement Control Station" monitoring the area for incoming aircraft or missiles. When a missile is spotted, a pair of Patriots is launched from a mobile launcher. A ground radar system mounted on a third mobile flatbed, in addition to the Patriot itself, receives reflected radar signals from the enemy target.

The Patriot then transmits the data to be processed by computers on the ground. The ground station repeatedly transmits an adjusted flight path to the Patriot in flight. If successful, the Patriot will intercept the enemy missile, and destroy it in the air. Sometimes it will only hit part of the missile and the explosive warhead of the Scud will fall to the ground and hit an area not in its original path but still cause deadly damage.

One citizen told his story to the local newspaper:

Between *the time the siren went off and the explosion, I didn't have time to put on my mask. Then the lights went out, and I couldn't even find* the mask. After the explosion a cloud of dust filled the whole apartment. I thought it was gas, and I didn't have my mask on.

I was lucky to be in the living room at the time and not in my tiny bedroom that doubled as my sealed room. The glass panes in the bedroom door blew through the protective plastic sheet. Pieces of glass were all over the bed where I would have been lying. The whole room sort of squeezed in. It looked like a whirlwind of glass.

Before the big blast hit, I heard some explosions and thought the missile was overshooting my street. It must have been the Patriots partially hitting the Scud. A few moments later came the big explosion. It rocked the whole building. A piece of glass slashed through my sweater and cut my arm.

Outside there was a smell of sulfur and explosives in the air. The neighbors were staggering out of their homes, hysterical with shock and fear. One house looked like it was almost completely blown apart—only the concrete frame was still standing. Ceramic roof tiles were scattered everywhere. Windows were blown out with their frames. The concrete roof of a garage crashed into the windshield of a new Oldsmobile.

Another woman was standing beside her shattered car trying to make a phone call on the mobile phone, while her daughter held up the antenna that had been ripped off.

Soon the streets were filled with neighbors, rescue workers and soldiers. The noise was terrible. There was the sound of ambulance sirens, burglar alarms that had been triggered by the explosion, people crying and rescue workers shouting orders.

In the middle of the pandemonium a shopkeeper replaced the smashed windows of her clothing store with a large cardboard sign that said, "In spite of Saddam, we are open for business as usual on Saturday night." [25]

Other times, the Patriot explodes the Scud in mid-air, creating a tremendous shower of light and flaming scraps of metal. Although the potential damage is reduced, the danger to civilians below still remains.

Negotiations over the installation of Patriot batteries on Israeli soil were taking place between the Israelis and Americans for months before the war. Delays caused Israelis to believe that the United States did not take Saddam Hussein at his word when he promised to bring Israel into the war by torching half the Jewish State. The Bush Administration believed that, because of Israel's low profile and the tremendous buildup of American troop force in the Gulf, Saddam would never launch a missile attack on Israel.

Those hopes were dashed when the first volley of missiles hit Israel on Thursday night, January 18th, 1991. When it became apparent that the Patriots could successfully intercept Iraqi Scuds over Saudi Arabia, four Patriot batteries were immediately airlifted to Israel. Within hours, the first battery was operational and monitoring the skies over Tel Aviv. The Israeli government and military authorities constantly reminded the population that the Patriots only offered a partial solution. They were shown to be correct when a few missiles slipped through the defense system, or when the Patriot only partially destroyed the Scud. Yet the number of successful interceptions caused the population to breathe a little easier, and an epidemic of "Patriot fever" broke out around the country.

One citizen observed the following:

After the siren went off, my curiosity won over my better judgment and I went outside. I heard the loud double boom and saw the bright streaks of light of the Patriots taking off into the sky. Then I saw a flash of orange-colored lightning burst through the clouds. 26

A sight like that brought a sigh of relief to all the residents of Tel Aviv and Haifa, areas particularly hard hit by Scud attacks. The next morning, citizens spontaneously came to the Patriot batteries and brought champagne, cakes and cookies to the American and Israeli soldiers manning the stations. After one attack in Tel Aviv, a US soldier in his army fatigues was seen dancing in a circle with men in a neighborhood that absorbed the missile without any loss to human life. A kibbutz invited some soldiers for a softball game, and the children crowded around the Americans to get their autographs. Billboards were plastered throughout Tel

Aviv proclaiming, *"Kulanu Patriotim"*—"We are all Patriots!"

US soldier with kibbutz children
after a softball game.

The Thirty Nine Lashes

◀
◀
◀
◀
◀
◀
◀
◀
◀
◀
◀

The following is an unofficial summary of Iraq's Scud attacks on Israel, based on Israel Defense Force accounts.

FRIDAY,   JANUARY 18,   2:00 A.M.

Eight missiles are fired at Israel. One hits a two-story residential building in the Tel Aviv area; another hits a factory. A third missile hits a structure near Haifa. Twelve people suffer light to moderate injuries.

SATURDAY,   JANUARY 19,   7:20 A.M.

Four missiles were fired at Israel. One missile strikes the center of the country near a residential building, another hits near the Tel Aviv exhibition grounds and a third hits the bomb shelter of a public building. The fourth does not reach Israel. Sixteen people are lightly injured by missile fragments and flying debris.

TUESDAY, JANUARY 22, 8:50 P.M.

One Scud hits Ramat Gan. A Patriot missile hits another Scud but fails to prevent it from landing. A two-story home collapses, four hundred apartments are damaged and many other buildings are heavily damaged. Three people die of heart attacks; ninety-six are injured, six seriously.

WEDNESDAY, JANUARY 23, 10:00 P.M.

A Scud fired at the Haifa area is intercepted by two Patriot missiles. Windows are shattered in many apartments; there are no reports of injuries.

FRIDAY, JANUARY 25, 6:00 P.M.

Eight Scuds are fired at Israel. Several Patriot missiles are launched successfully intercepting some of the Scuds. Two neighborhoods in the Ramat Gan area take direct hits. One hundred forty-four apartments are heavily damaged; four hundred others incur light to moderate damage. A two-story house collapses; an entire family is rescued from the rubble. One man is killed and forty-five people are injured, one seriously.

SATURDAY, JANUARY 26, 10:00 P.M.

Four Scuds fired at Israel are intercepted by Patriots. Debris from three of the Scuds fired at Haifa causes windows to shatter in several northern settlements. The fourth launched at the Dan region causes no damage or casualties.

MONDAY, JANUARY 28, 9:00 P.M.

A Scud lands near the village of Dir Balut in the territories. No injuries or damage are reported.

THURSDAY, JANUARY 31, 6:00 P.M.

A Scud hits the territories. No injuries or damage.

SATURDAY, FEBRUARY 2, 8:30 P.M.

A Scud hits an unsettled part of the territories. No injuries or damage.

SUNDAY, FEBRUARY 3, 1:40 A.M.

A second Scud fired the same night falls, like the earlier one, in the territories. No injuries or damage.

FRIDAY, FEBRUARY 8, 2:40 A.M.

A Scud hits a neighborhood in the center of the country. More than 400 apartments are damaged by the attack. Twenty-five people are injured.

MONDAY, FEBRUARY 11, 6:52 P.M.

A Scud lands in an uninhabited area in the center of Israel. No injuries or damage.

TUESDAY, FEBRUARY 12, 1:30 A.M.

A Scud hits a residential area in the center of the country. One house is completely destroyed and windows in dozens of other homes are shattered. According to a US State Department spokesman, the missile lands near the residence of Defense Minister Moshe Arens. Six residents are injured.

SATURDAY, FEBRUARY 16, 8:05 P.M.

Two Scuds are launched in a coordinated attack. For the first time, one lands in the south of the country in an open area. Parts of the other fall into the sea in the north of the country. No injuries or damage result from either missile.

TUESDAY, FEBRUARY 19, 8:00 P.M.

A Scud lands in an open area in the center of the country. No injuries or damage.

SATURDAY, FEBRUARY 23, 6:50 P.M.

A Scud lands in an unpopulated area in the center of the country, where it ignites a fire. No injuries or damage.

MONDAY, FEBRUARY 25, 3:37 A.M.

A Scud lands in an unpopulated area in the south of Israel. No injuries or damage.

MONDAY, FEBRUARY 25, 5:36 A.M.

In the second Scud attack of the morning, a missile lands in an unpopulated area in the south of Israel. No injuries or damage.

The following list represents official estimates of damages and casualties caused by the thirty-nine Scud missiles fired at Israel:

1) 4,095 buildings are damaged; this includes 3,991 apartments and residential buildings, 331 public institutions, 17 educational institutions and 54 businesses.

2) 1,644 families are evacuated in the area of Tel Aviv and Ramat Gan.

3) 230 people are injured from the force of a Scud blast; 220 are lightly injured, 9 moderately injured and 1 person is severely injured. Sixty people required hospitalization; most were released the next day.

4) 12 deaths result indirectly from the missile attacks.

5) 1 person is killed by a missile.[27]

It is easy to look at the statistics and be overjoyed that so few people have been killed or injured during Scud missile attacks. When one considers that based on what happened during similar attacks on Teheran during the Iran-Iraq war, that Israeli authorities were planning to handle thousands of dead and injured civilians, it becomes easy to see only the salvation. But in a small country like Israel, every casualty is a tragedy felt deeply by the entire nation. Even though the victims are whole on the outside, no one knows the suffering they and their families will have to undergo in the years to come.

The son of the only person to die as a direct result of a missile attack expressed his grief this way.

Don't let anyone tell me that they understand what I am feeling. Not that I would feel any better if my father was killed together with another 200 people in the attack, but that is what everyone is saying, "Only one person was killed!" For me it wasn't only one person. It was my one father—a one hundred percent loss.[28]

PART III

Masks

Conventional, Gas Or Worse?

◄ *January 24, 1991*

In the geriatric department of Ichilov hospital, a seventy-eight year old man waited for an operation to reset his broken leg.

The old man is Menachem Begin.

On the night of the first Scud attack, gathered together with the other elderly patients in the sealed hospital room, no one recognized the face of the former Prime Minister behind his gas mask.

Menachem Begin served as Prime Minister of Israel from 1977 to 1983. Even if people in the hospital did recognize him, how many would have realized that the miracle of so few injuries from the missile attacks was partially due to a courageous and fateful decision made by Prime Minister Begin in 1981.

Prime Minister Begin had received numerous intelligence reports indicating that Saddam Hussein was preparing a nuclear bomb. In response, Begin ordered the Iraqi nuclear reactor at Osirak destroyed and the

Israeli Air Force successfully carried out that order. The world community was shocked and reacted with universal condemnation of Israel for the attack. Now, as the Gulf War raged, the international coalition was relieved that they only had to contend with conventional, gas or biological warheads. If just one of the Scuds that hit Tel Aviv had been armed with a nuclear warhead, the entire city could have been erased from the map.

Before the war started, the Israeli Civil Defense authorities confronted a serious dilemma: Should they prepare the population for a conventional missile attack or a chemical attack? In the case of a conventional attack, the best safeguard is a standard bomb shelter built of reinforced concrete. (In Israel, bomb shelters are located in the basement of most buildings, public and private.) On the other hand, in the event of a chemical attack, bomb shelters would not provide adequate protection. Poison gas sinks to the ground and is able to enter through cracks and seams between door and window frames. The bomb shelters were not made to keep out seeping poison gases. In the case of such an attack, the safest place to be is in a sealed room as high above ground level as possible. Additionally, even if the shelters could be properly sealed, since the speed of the Scud missiles leaves little time for warning and reaction, it is likely that many families would never make it to the communal shelters in time.

We have also learned lessons from Saddam's previous conventional Scud attacks on Iran and his use of chemical weapons against his own Kurdish population. The conventional bombs leave ten to twenty people dead after each attack. The chemical attacks leave hundreds dead in their wake. Saddam had promised to strike at Israel with poison gas, and he had already delivered on every one of his promises. No matter what else he lied about, when it came to killing Jews, Saddam Hussein could be trusted.

Eventually the Army decided to go with the sealed rooms, and the country was informed of the decision. With each citizen wearing a gas mask in a sealed room, the threat of the mass murder of civilians by poison gas in any attack would be greatly reduced. Yet horrible memories of the Holocaust are dragged up at the mere mention of poison gas. Many had lost relatives and friends in the gas chambers of the Nazi death camps.

Many others are Holocaust survivors themselves, as Rebecca relates below:

After experiencing what we've been through, it's hard to frighten us with the current situation. A lot of the younger people are running away to Jerusalem or the south, but we're staying here. We're tired of running. We don't want to pack up and move again. We ran away and wandered—with suitcases, without suitcases—our whole lives we've wandered until we got here. We don't want to hide anymore. I know that my time could be up at any moment and any place. When you confront death face to face so many times, it's hard not to become a fatalist. I don't know why I was saved and my sister not; why my friend in the next bunk died and I lived. The only thing I know is that it's not in our hands. At times like these, you have to believe in Providence.

So I guess I'm calm, I'm not afraid of Saddam, and I don't get excited about the sirens. The only thing that bothers me is that they have "Zyklon B"—the same gas the Germans used to kill my whole family. Of my twenty-five cousins, only four survived. I can't begin to count how many of my other relatives died in the gas chambers.[29]

People line up quietly to receive their protective kits: A gas mask, purifying powder and pads in case some drops of chemical touches their skin, and a self-injecting atropine syringe filed with an antidote that counteracts the frightening and deadly symptoms of nerve gas.

Thirty Scuds have landed bearing conventional warheads and many citizens have started to ignore Civil Defense instructions and have gone to bomb shelters instead of sealed rooms. After seeing the tremendous scenes of destruction, they were afraid to depend on the miracles that had allowed sheets of plastic to protect their friends and acquaintances from the fury of the Scuds.

Some people have come up with a solution that involves going to the stairwell in the center of their building when the siren goes off, and then after the explosions have subsided, they return to their sealed room—if it is still standing. A number of people saved their lives this way. Others decided to stay in their sealed rooms only to see their stair wells demolished.

In the end, Israeli Civil Defense came up with a compromise solution. Those with a shelter inside their private homes were to seal it off and use it for their sealed room. Those who could reach a sealed bomb shelter within two minutes could use it, unless it would be difficult to find, such as at night when people are awakened from sleep. Otherwise, it was best to continue using the sealed rooms.

In fact, there was no best defense. No one could be sure what Saddam's next move would be.

Faces Behind The Mask

◄ **January 25, 1991**

By 1985 Syria and Iraq had acquired the capability to launch missiles deep inside Israeli territory.

Israel then began to prepare for a nightmare scenario—poison gas attacks.

During the 1980's, Israel's neighbors began arming themselves with missiles.

Syria, Saudi Arabia and Iraq all installed surface-to-surface missile batteries capable of reaching Israel's major cities. Both Syria and Iraq possessed chemical weapons. As a result, the Israeli Army began a campaign to prepare for the unthinkable—a poisonous gas attack on its civilian population centers.

The need to develop personal protection kits for every man, woman and child in the country has presented unprecedented logistical problems. Conventional masks designed for soldiers are far too big to create a seal around a child's face. Even if miniature versions of these masks could be produced, how could you keep a four year-old from ripping off her mask? The masks are hot and uncomfortable to wear. And what about someone with asthma?

Israeli engineers have come up with a number of creative solutions. Miniature, portable plastic tents with built-in filters have been designed to accommodate babies up to three years of age. Small children up to age six have been provided with a see-through plastic hood and battery-operated blower so that they won't feel so hot and confined. Older children have received miniature versions of their parents' gas masks.

Everyone, including children, have carrying cases to take their gas masks wherever they go.

In the weeks before January 15, 1991, an organized campaign took place that distributed personal protective kits to over three million people. Distribution centers were set up in school buildings and community centers. Families came together to be fitted with their masks and to receive instructions on how to use the equipment. Yet, despite all the organization, not all eventualities could have been anticipated.

When the siren sounded in the first missile attack on January 18, the nurses in the neonatal intensive care unit in a downtown Jerusalem hospital pulled the premature babies out of their incubators and placed them in the plastic tents. Unfortunately, because of the babies under developed temperature regulatory system, they began to turn blue. That, coupled with the risk of infection, meant that the protective tent created more problems than it solved.

The head of one neonatal department took the problem to her husband, a researcher in gas exchange. From the Civil Defense, he procured one of the air pumps and filters used in the gas masks for young children. He then sealed all the openings to an incubator except for one hole, into which he inserted the plastic pipe attached to the pump and filter. Within days, preemie incubators were being turned into mini-sealed rooms—complete with the standard brown sealing tape—thus eliminating the need to move the tiny infants. This has quickly become standard procedure in preemie wards around the country.[30]

In the meantime, the regular rooms where newborn infants are kept in bassinets, are totally filled by the regular-sized baby gas tents. As a result, the Army has developed a mini-tent with a motorized blower to eliminate overheating.

Gas masks have been designed to ensure an airtight seal against the wearer's face. This has presented a special problem for eyeglass wearers who have to remove their glasses in order to put their masks on. A number of companies in Israel have responded with mini-glasses that fit under masks. Another company has devised a different solution by providing lenses that can be attached to the outside of the mask.

An even greater danger exists for the blind, who have to find and put on their masks, and enter and seal their rooms in the two minutes allotted to the sighted population.

A gas proof tent designed for newborn infants is demonstrated for a group of Ethiopian mothers.

One couple shared this experience:

My wife is blind, and I have a ninety-percent loss of vision. During each alarm, I have to help my wife put her gas mask on. Each time she becomes hysterical, and it takes two days to calm her down.

This last attack came in the middle of the night. I woke her up and she immediately started to scream again. I forced the mask on her and dragged her to our sealed room. I hugged her until we heard the explosions. The last one was so strong that it sent us flying to opposite corners of the room. Because of the shock, it took me a few minutes to get up and I couldn't see her because of the smoke. I shouted, "Shula, where are you, where are you? But she didn't answer. I was sure she was dead. I ran around the house feeling with my hands, falling and bumping into things, trying to work out what part of the house I was in. I know my way around by touch and by the way the furniture is arranged. But because the blast had turned everything over, I couldn't figure out where I was.

Suddenly, I heard a terrible scream and I felt I was stepping on a living body. I had accidentally stepped on my poor wife, who had tried to crawl by touch and find me or the entrance of the house. I called out to her, "Shula, it's me, it's me, " and I tried to hug her but she was hysterical. She probably didn't realize it was me. Then I heard the sounds of rescuers. I called out to them and they got me out. While we sat outside covered in blankets, my wife said to me suddenly, "This is the first time I'm glad that I'm blind. I don't want to see our house, in which we've invested twenty years of our lives, in ruins."[31]

The population has been ordered to carry their gas masks wherever they go. The kits come in a drab cardboard box with a built-in plastic carrying strap. To help eliminate the doom and gloom brought to mind by the familiar boxes, people began decorating them. Children are still passing away the hours busily coloring and pasting pictures to the outside of their boxes. Transient artists who normally sell jewelry on the street are hawking colorful replacement boxes made out of corrugated sheets of plastic. One enterprising person in the religious community marketed an attractive wraparound cover for the gas mask box decorated with relevant Biblical verses. All proceeds are going to charity, of course.

The speed of the Scud missile gives people little time to take cover. Those at special risk are people traveling on highways in their cars. Civil Defense authorities have issued special instructions to those who find themselves in automobiles when the alarm is sounded.

Everyone has received the following instructions:

All *drivers and passengers must keep their gas mask kits close at hand while traveling. When an alert is sounded in an open area, drivers should pull over, turn off the engine, and don the mask. If there is no nearby shelter, the car windows and vents should be securely closed and one should pay close attention to radio announcements.*[32]

In theory, the instructions made sense. In practice, when the missiles actually fell, the procedure was somewhat different.

One motorist put it like this:

Our house was seriously damaged during the first attack. Luckily, at the time of the explosion, neither of us was home. We couldn't take the tension so we decided to visit some friends out of town. We got into our car and headed north. On the way, we heard the siren and then the explosion. The windows of the car blew out and a piece of the missile came in through the tailgate and exited through the right-hand door, flying inches past my wife's head. My mother-in-law was in the back seat, and she was uninjured as well.[33]

The deaf and hard of hearing have a special problem, especially if they live at home alone. They can't hear the sirens. A number of companies are renting special cordless vibrating beepers, that are activated whenever an alert or all-clear is sounded. It is a welcome tool for many who, since the beginning of the war, suffer from fear of sleeping through a missile attack.

Shlomo and Chava, who are deaf, related this story:

Both my wife and I are deaf, so at the beginning of the war, I set my alarm clock to go off every two hours, in order to see if we were sleeping through a missile attack. The alarm is attached to an intense strobe light that flashes to wake me up. The only problem is, it takes only five minutes from the time the sirens go off until the missiles land. Now we take turns watching the TV all night long waiting for the "alarm" sign to show up on the screen. Since we can't hear the announcements on the radio, sometimes we sit for an extra half hour with our masks on until the "all-clear" sign comes on for the entire country. The whole crisis is much more frightening when you don't know what is happening around you.[34]

The Russians Are Coming— Still?

January 26, 1991

For over twenty years, Jews around the world fought for the right of their brethren to escape the religious persecution and tyranny of the Soviet Union.

Throughout the seventies and eighties, mass demonstrations were staged against the Soviet regime to free the Prisoners of Zion (Jews who wanted to emigrate to Israel but were denied visas by the Soviet government). Around the world people rallied to free the jailed *Refuseniks* (those whose request for a visa had been refused, and whose only crime was the desire to emigrate and settle in Israel). Because of government restrictions, it was virtually impossible to openly practice Judaism in the Soviet Union. Prayer books and Bibles had to be smuggled into the country by western visitors. Hebrew lessons were held clandestinely. Sabbath candles were kindled with the shades drawn tight so that no one could see them from the outside.

Since that time, the unbelievable has occurred. The Soviets surrendered to the West and ended the Cold

War. The Berlin Wall came down. And then the gates opened for Soviet Jews to emigrate. In 1990, almost two hundred thousand Russian immigrants arrived in Israel. By December, the ingathering of the exiles reached a rate of one thousand five hundred per day. It was a virtual nonstop airlift of Jews returning to their homeland.

At the same time, each day that new immigrants arrived in Israel was also one day closer to another war in the Middle East. As the January 15, UN deadline for Iraq to pull out of Kuwait approached, and with it the threat of war, many expected a halt in the immigration to Israel. Remarkably, even after January 17, when the U.S.-led coalition began its bombardment of the Iraqi military, plane loads of new Jewish arrivals continue to land in Israel. Most airlines have canceled their flights to the Middle East, but El Al (Israel's national airline) continues to bring home plane load after plane load of Russian Jews. Though there has been a slowdown, immigrants continue to arrive at a rate of five hundred per day. Some, by any means available.

David and Miriam told their story to a reporter:

My wife and I, our two children and my parents, drove to Israel from Chernobyl in our Lada carrying all our possessions behind us in a trailer. We arrived at the port of Haifa on January 14. The authorities gave us gas masks and a check for initial expenses. We then went to visit some friends in Kiryat Motzkin, but there was no room for all of us to sleep in the apartment. We spent the night in the car. Before the authorities were able to help us find a home, the Gulf

War began. For the first few days, every time there was an alert, we went into the car, put on our masks and closed all the doors and windows. We knew there was a chance of war before we came, but we don't regret coming. We are not afraid of gas because we have the masks. At Chernobyl we didn't have masks. When we returned to the authorities they were surprised, as they thought we must have already found accommodations during the attacks. They immediately arranged a temporary apartment for us. [35]

As they come down the ramp from the plane, many of the new arrivals bend down and kiss the ground; such are the feelings of Jews returning to their home. Sadly, the first gift they receive upon their arrival in the Promised Land is a gas mask. Many of the immigrants go to visit friends and relatives who have already settled in their own homes. Most of them choose to live in the center of the country —some in Ramat Gan.

Home at last. Russian Jews are welcomed at Ben Gurion airport.

Helena and Efim are typical of the thousands
of Russian immigrants.
Their story is a familiar one:

We were staying in a neighborhood in southern
Tel Aviv during the first missile attack,
visiting with other Russian immigrants who were living
in the area. Many of the people in the poorer houses of
the neighborhood had not bothered to prepare a sealed
room, so when the siren went off we all rushed to the
nearby public bomb shelter. The shelter was huge and it
was located inside a large building made of concrete and
metal.

About two hundred people gathered together to seek
shelter inside the formidable building. A number of us
moved to the wall on the eastern side of the shelter. If
required, that side of the shelter served as a synagogue
(because it faced Jerusalem) and the wall was filled with
prayer books, Bibles and other holy books. People were
reciting Psalms over the sound of crying babies. And
then came the explosion. Everything came crashing
down around us. The shelter had taken a direct hit by a
missile carrying five hundred and fifty pounds of
explosives. There was a smell of burning sulfur, and a
thick cloud of dust filled the room.

Some of the people were thrown into the air. Others
had thrown themselves to the ground and were
screaming wildly. When the noise stopped and the dust

began to clear, the people who had been frozen in shock began to get up and look around. Everyone was totally astonished to see that not one of the two hundred people was injured!

The building had totally collapsed, including three walls of the shelter. Only the eastern wall facing Jerusalem remained standing. The books and the bookshelves were untouched.

The next morning Prime Minister Shamir visited the area with the Mayor of Tel Aviv. Mr. Shamir asked in astonishment if there had really been people in the shelter at the time of the attack. Mayor Lahat answered that indeed there were two hundred, and all were saved by a miracle.[36]

Although every effort was made to facilitate a smooth and comfortable transition for the immigrants, the stress from being uprooted from their native country and being thrust into the middle of a war was too much for some. Two Soviet immigrants died of heart attacks when the sirens sounded on January 18. The assistance of neighbors and veteran immigrants helped many newcomers to cope with and survive the war.

This is Raiza's story:

I arrived on December 29 with my daughter, son-in-law and two grandchildren from Leningrad. We have been staying with relatives since January 15.

They are also from Leningrad, but they arrived here in October 1973 during the Yom Kippur War. The courage of people here, and their assurance that things will get better, has astonished me. You feel protected here, that somebody is watching over you. You never feel like that in the Soviet Union. In the Soviet Union we also had civil defense, and every six months or so we would go and try on gas masks. But there the masks are so old and worn that you can't even wear them for five minutes, and they don't have them for everybody. It adds to the feeling that you are on your own. Here it is different.

I have to admit that the hours we spent in the sealed room during the attacks were very frightening. There were thirteen of us together. Sitting in the room, I thought of World War II. I was four years old in 1941, and it brought back horrible memories. A mother of five with whom I've become friendly calmed me down after the first attack by saying, "Everything will be all right, God will protect us." This woman also told me she was able to sleep after the sirens went off. I was up all night. I was astounded that a mother of five wasn't afraid of war. Maybe I will also be calm in a couple of years when I understand the situation as well as the Israelis.[37]

Perhaps the strangest welcome for a group of new immigrants occurred even before they arrived. An El Al plane carrying Russian immigrants was approaching Ben Gurion Airport when the sirens went off. The plane was allowed to continue on its path but had to circle until air traffic controllers gave it permission to land after the attack.[38]

Despite the danger and an initial downturn in immigration from the Soviet Union, the number of people seeking visas to Israel at the consulate in Moscow reached three to four thousand requests per week by the third week of the war.

One young man reflected:

I want to go now rather than later, so I can make a contribution to my country. My mother begged me to wait, but I told her that it would be dishonorable. I will be leaving for Israel as soon as I get my visa.[39]

The enthusiasm expressed by those still in the Soviet Union waiting to emigrate to Israel was echoed by those who were already there—no matter how trying their experiences were.

This is how another new immigrant put it:

I arrived in Israel eight months ago, and after a lot of effort we found this apartment to rent. Last night, when we heard the siren, I jumped out of bed and ran to the living room. Minutes later, after having been hit, our bedroom was a pile of rubble. We were all unhurt.

I've been cleaning up broken glass all morning. This morning when some photographers and journalists

walked by below, I hung up the little plastic Israeli flag
they gave us at the airport when we first arrived. That's
Israel—missiles or no missiles, it's still better than
Russia.[40]

Elderly immigrants being led away from
what's left of their new home in Tel Aviv.

Sadly, It's A Small World Too

◀◀◀◀◀◀◀◀◀◀◀◀◀◀◀◀

January 27, 1991

The children are the most heartbreaking victims of the war.

The anguish of having to awaken sleepy children in the middle of the night and force them to put on rubber masks covered with plastic bags, or to push infants through the small opening of plastic tents, is indescribable.

The outrage is even greater when they suffer physically from the attacks.

Danni and Reva described their feelings to a reporter:

We were asleep and didn't hear the alarm. At 2:00 a.m. the blast of an explosion woke us up. We ran to the children's room. There, we saw that pieces of plaster had fallen from the ceiling. We took the kids into the sealed room. Later, when we emerged after the all clear signal, we found a gaping hole in the ceiling of the children's room. The table and chairs had been totally demolished. We realized that a miracle had occurred; nothing had happened to the children. We're still finding it hard to believe.[41]

The traditional Friday night Sabbath meal is something almost every Israeli child looks forward to. It doesn't matter how religious a family is or isn't, Friday nights are special. Gathering the whole family together for a festive dinner and songs has always provided a warm sense of security for Jewish children through the ages. Now, Saddam had robbed the children of even that small pleasure.

One grandmother summed things up like this:

O*n Friday night the children and grandchildren came over for supper. Even before we had managed to do anything, the siren went off. We ran directly to the sealed room. The grandchildren began to cry and scream, and we barely managed to put their gas masks on. They were hysterical and shaking all over. Then the missile landed, shaking the entire area. I heard the walls of the house cave in. The door flew off, and nothing was left in its place. Glass was everywhere, and the entrance to the veranda was blocked with rubble.*

We couldn't go outside because the exit was blocked. As we were waiting for the rescue team, I looked at the grandchildren in order to calm them down, and I saw their faces covered in blood. I nearly fainted, because I didn't know how badly they were hurt. We cleaned their faces, and it turned out that they had only been scratched from pieces of flying glass. Yesterday I felt sorry for the victims. Today, we are the victims.[42]

Children whose homes have been destroyed or severely damaged have found themselves temporarily living in a resort hotel provided by the government. It might be fun to play in the hallways, but it is not the ideal environment for an eight-year-old to recover from the shock of seeing her house, and the houses of her friends, destroyed.

Eight-year-old Sara told her family's story:

We came from the Soviet Union five months ago. Since the explosion, my father has been very nervous. He's been screaming a lot, and my mother panics every time there is an alarm. But I'm not scared. When the alarm goes off, I walk with them down the hall to the sealed room. All my friends from the neighborhood are there.[43]

Many children, especially those who live through attacks, suffer from anxiety, nervousness, insomnia and headaches.

One sixteen year old described his
experience this way.

I was so nervous after the United Nations deadline
passed on January 15 that I couldn't sleep for
three straight nights. On the night of the 18th, I decided
to take a late-night bath to help me go to sleep. It was
2:00 A.M. when the siren went off. At first I thought I'd
heard an ambulance passing by. When I realized after a
few seconds that it was actually an air raid alarm, I
rinsed myself off, grabbed a towel and ran to the sealed
room. Since then I've developed a new symptom of the
war, bath-aphobia.[44]

The entire national school system has been forced to
shut down since the war broke out. For security
reasons, children are kept close to their sealed rooms
at home. Eventually people will go back to work, but
the schools remain closed; as a result one parent must
always stay home from work to care for the children.
Against mounting pressure, the Ministry of Education,
in conjunction with Civil Defense, did reopen the
schools under strict guidelines. Classrooms have been
sealed, and adult volunteers are on hand to help
children put on their masks if necessary. Daily "missile
drills" make sure that everyone gets the gas masks on
in time.

This is how Jerry sees things:

I remember growing up in America in the 1960's during the peak of the Cold War. Every so often we would have "nuclear drills." Thirty little kids would put their hands behind their heads and hide under their desks. It was a little ridiculous. Now I worried, as I watched my own little girl go off to school, struggling under the weight of the gas mask slung over her shoulder. For her, each gas mask drill at school caused her to relive the terror of the real attack that happened the night before.[45]

A gas mask drill in school.

The severe disruption of daily routines makes coping and adjustment difficult for the children. Further confusion develops when sirens sound and children are forced to put on their gas masks and go into a sealed room to hide from a danger no one can see. Worst of all are the false alarms—they add another dimension to the stress and anxiety. The air is filled with feelings of fear, confusion, resentment and dread. The difficulties are enormously compounded when a small child has the misfortune of crossing paths with a Scud.

This is the voice of one parent:

After the ordeal of the first siren that night, my four-year-old son seemed to settle down a little bit. When the second siren went off, he woke up hysterical. "Mommy, you promised," he screamed, "You promised there wouldn't be any more sirens! It's your fault. It's your fault." It was a false alarm, and I quickly got him back to bed.

The third siren went off in the middle of the night and woke me up. Before I could get out of bed to go and wake him up, he ran into my room, jumped onto the bed and started hitting me with his fists. "You're a liar, you're a liar!" He was crying hysterically. "It's all your fault. You said there wouldn't be any more missiles."

All of a sudden, we heard a tremendous explosion, and all the glass around us shattered. His face was cut by flying glass and he froze in panic. I picked him up and we ran outside. When he saw our neighbor's house demolished, he went into shock and started shaking. I couldn't calm him down. Two hours later I still couldn't get him to speak. He won't move and he won't respond to anything I say.[46]

Growing Arab Support In Israel— For Saddam!

January, 28 1991

It's been said that the Palestinian Arabs have never missed an opportunity to miss an opportunity.

The support by the Palestinians of Saddam Hussein during the missile attacks has almost been as baffling as the stories of survival from the attacks themselves. At a time when the whole world is united against Saddam Hussein, and the whole world is calculating the punishment to be inflicted on him and his supporters after the war, the Palestinians are siding with him, further fueling their hatred of Israel.

The following report appeared in a major Israeli newspaper.

O*n hearing the siren Friday night, residents of Tulkarm went up to the roofs of their houses, shouting "Allah is great," and calling on Saddam*

Hussein to continue attacking Tel Aviv. They whistled cries of victory. The shouts of victory grew louder when flashes of the explosions were seen [hitting the Jewish neighborhoods]. Despite the inclement weather, men, women and children climbed onto the roofs of their houses, yelling out cries of support. "Keep up the bombing!" and "Send another one, Saddam!" were among the cries that could be heard. Shouts of support and cries of, "Jihad against the Americans," were broadcast from mobile loudspeakers and from speakers atop local mosques. Similar shouting could be heard throughout the territories, even in places like Hebron that have so far not expressed their support of the attacks against Israel. Residents of Hebron stated that immediately after the siren, many people switched off the lights of their homes, went up to the rooftops and called out cries of joy and victory.[47]

Another reporter contacted Palestinian Arabs in the territories after the second missile attack on Tel Aviv and reported the following comments.

Y*ou [Jews] deserve it. Saddam gave his word and kept it. He's not forgetting the Palestinians.* You aren't immune from Iraq's missiles. This, with minor variations, was the message I was given in almost every phone call I made.

A resident of Tulkarm said, "*Right after the sirens were sounded, we heard members of the popular committees of the uprising calling out on their hand-held loudspeakers: "Be careful! Saddam's attack on the Jews has begun." At first we were not afraid, but then when we heard the reverberation of the explosions, we woke the children up and understood that it was missiles. We turned on the radio and heard what happened. We love Saddam Hussein. We loved him before he bombed Israel, and now we love him even more."*

A PLO youth leader in Kalandiya said, in a pronounced display of elation and contentment, *"Now we are waiting for Saddam Hussein to bomb Tel Aviv with chemical weapons."*

"People in the refugee camp are satisfied. They're saying, 'Israel's about to go under.' When we heard the siren, people came out and shouted in the streets 'Allah akbar—God is great.' What are we satisfied about? It is the first time since 1948 that Tel Aviv has been bombed, and it proves that Saddam Hussein stands by his commitment to protect the Palestinians."

For the past few days, residents of the territories have been sitting at home glued to their radios and television sets. However, their listening and viewing habits have changed. Rather than tuning in to the Voice of Israel's Arabic-language news service as they have in the past, now Jordan's radio and television broadcasts have become exceedingly popular. *"Radio Jordan is broadcasting true reports now. Saudi Arabia, Syria, and Israel are transmitting unreliable propaganda,"* I have been told. The explanation: "*Radio Jordan lauds and praises the bombing of Tel Aviv and demonstrates support for Saddam Hussein.*"

There are, however, more sober voices among the leaders in the territories. "*I'm sorry we're rejoicing in this fashion,*" one prominent figure from Nablus told me. "*In the final analysis, we know Saddam Hussein will be routed. We Palestinians, who supported him all the way, will pay the price of defeat.*"[48]

"Scud fever" has broken out across the river in Jordan. Scud lapel pins, Scud postcards, Scud key chains and Scud-shaped birthday cakes are being gobbled up by the kingdom's one-and-a-half-million Palestinian residents. Large colored posters of Jordan's King Hussein handing an automatic rifle to Saddam Hussein in front of Jerusalem's Temple Mount have also become a big seller.

On January 23, the Mufti of Jerusalem, the leading Moslem religious leader in the country, called for Jihad (holy war) against the United States and its allies. He denounced America as the number one enemy of Islam and Moslems. The Popular Front for the Liberation of Palestine issued a statement calling on "the people of the region to attack American interests and to put an end to the American-Zionist aggression against the Arab nation."

When Yasir Arafat was interviewed on CNN and asked how he felt about Israel's lack of retaliation against the Scud missile attacks, he responded, "What do you mean? The only reason Scuds are being fired on Israel is because they launched Tomahawk cruise missiles on Baghdad first!"

From Babylon To Jerusalem And Back

◀ **January 31, 1991**

The establishment of the modern-day State of Israel in 1948 was followed by a massive airlift of Jews from Arab countries throughout the Middle East.

This historic return to their homeland liberated over 300,000 Jews from centuries of anti-Semitism and persecution. Virtually the entire Jewish population of Iraq was brought to Israel between 1948 and 1950. Today, only six hundred Jews still remain in Iraq.

Operation *Ezra and Nechemia* (named for the Jewish prophets who were exiled to, and later returned from, ancient Babylon) transported over one hundred and twenty thousand men, women and children from Iraq to Israel. Many of these Iraqi Jews were resettled in Tel Aviv, and ironically one of the first neighborhoods to suffer a Scud attack was a community of Jews originally from Baghdad. In fact, of the total population of one hundred and fifty thousand in Ramat Gan (the first neighborhood hit in Tel Aviv), forty thousand are Iraqi Jews. Ramat Gan Mayor Zvi Bar, who is also of Iraqi Kurdish descent, was heard saying that perhaps that is why Saddam had it in for Ramat Gan.

One twenty-year-old immigrant came from northern Iraq. Three years earlier, he had been living in a Kurdish village where he witnessed the horror of Saddam's poisonous gas attacks on his own citizens.

My family moved from a town outside of Baghdad to a small village in Kurdistan while I was still a young boy. We hid the fact that we were Jews and blended in with the rest of the Kurds. When I was a teenager, I was drafted into the Kurdish resistance movement. One day, three years ago, I and some fellow fighters got into a skirmish with some Iraqi soldiers trying to climb up a steep mountain. We managed to drive them off.

We were on our way home when we heard the planes coming. We reached a hill overlooking the village and saw the planes drop their bombs. There was black smoke when the bombs hit. After that we couldn't see anything else. Some of us wanted to run down to see what had happened, but the older fighters knew what had happened and stopped us. They made us wait four hours, and then they had us circle the village and approach it from upwind.

The veterans told us to tear off pieces of our clothing and wet them with water. That's what we used to cover our faces. When we entered the village we found three hundred people dead or dying. We helped those who could be helped. There were no sirens, no sealed rooms, no masks and no medical help. Luckily, my family was out of the village tending the orchards. Afterwards we made our way out of Iraq and arrived in Israel seven months ago.[49]

Just north of the Kuwaiti border, near the banks of the Euphrates River, lies the ancient city of Ur in the region of Kasdim. Ur is one of the oldest archaeological sites in the world. It is located in an area that historians refer to as "the cradle of civilization." Three weeks into the war, U.S. military intelligence sighted Iraqi troops dug in around the archaeological sites at Ur and saw MIG fighter jets hidden among the ruins. Apparently, Saddam was depending on the Americans to be more civilized than he was.

The Jewish people trace their origins back to this ancient city of Ur.

Four thousand years ago, in that same city of Ur, a man named Abraham left his father's home and began his journey along the banks of the Euphrates River and across the Fertile Crescent until he reached what is now northern Israel. There, he gazed out at the land that would become the home of his descendants, the Jewish people. After the experience of slavery in Egypt, the Exodus and the crossing of the Red Sea, the Jews wandered through the Sinai Desert for forty years until finally settling in the land of their forefather, Abraham. King David established Jerusalem as the capital of the new kingdom, and his son, King Solomon, built the First Temple on Mount Moriah in the tenth century BCE. The Temple was a symbol of peace for all humanity. Jerusalem prospered and shared its prosperity with other countries. Ideally situated at the crossroads of three continents, it flourished as a trading center. Caravans traversed the country from Egypt, Babylon and every other civilized nation.

In the seventh century BCE, the Babylonians conquered the Assyrian empire in Mesopotamia. Under the regime of Nebuchadnezzar, Babylonia was built into the most powerful empire in the world. Nebuchadnezzar ruthlessly attacked his neighbors, annexed them to his own land and extended the reaches of his mighty empire.

Early in the sixth century BCE, Nebuchdnezzar's army invaded Israel. It met little resistance and quickly ravaged the country. Solomon's Temple was destroyed, and Jerusalem and her holy sites were defiled and pillaged. The conquered Jews became the victims of unspeakable atrocities. The population was taken captive and exiled to Babylon, along with their treasures of gold and priceless religious artifacts. Nebuchadnezzar used the wealth he plundered from his neighbors to reward and support his army and to build magnificent monuments to his own glory. In his own capital, he built the legendary Hanging Gardens of Babylon, one of the wonders of the ancient world. As a striking testimony to his personal grandeur, Nebuchadnezzar ordered that each brick used in the construction of the Hanging Gardens be inscribed with his name. It was this exile to Persia that moved the prophet to lament, "By the rivers of Babylon, the Children of Israel sat and wept, and remembered Zion."[50]

North of the ancient city of Ur, also on the Euphrates River, lies the biblical city of Babylon. Years ago, Saddam Hussein commissioned archaeologists to restore its ancient beauty, including the Hanging Gardens. Each new brick that was added was again inscribed with a ruler's, only this time it was the name of Saddam Hussein. For Saddam, this became a powerful symbol. Saddam believed that he was a reincarnation of the great Nebuchadnezzar and dreamed of restoring the Babylonian empire to its former size and glory. During the course of the restoration, archaeologists uncovered a plaque on the right-hand side of the ancient city gate that had been placed there by Nebuchadnezzar. This plaque bore a proclamation extolling the ancient ruler's greatness. Saddam ordered stonemasons to install another plaque directly across from the original, on the left-hand side of the gate. This plaque speaks of the greatness of Saddam Hussein. With his national symbol in place, Saddam embarked on a campaign of terror—first in Iran and then in Kuwait. Ultimately, he dreamed of recapturing Jerusalem.

A few hundred miles away, in one of Jerusalem's religious neighborhoods, life continues as before.

Though sealed rooms had been prepared, the believers who populate this community are confident that Jerusalem will not be harmed.

One devout Jew put it this way.

This war is different. Now it is clear that it is only the evil from Babylon that is trying to attack us. The Torah tells us in the prophecies that we will be protected this time. Instead of Jerusalem, it will be Saddam Hussein and his country that will be destroyed. Here, let me show you.

Most people are familiar with the beginning of Psalm 137, which reads: "By the rivers of Babylon, there we sat, and we wept, when we remembered Zion." Few people are familiar with the end of the Psalm: "O daughter of Babylon, marked for devastation; happy is he who shall repay you in measure for what you have done to us." It seems to be saying that the nation that will come after Babylon ("daughter of Babylon") will be destroyed, like Nebuchadnezzar destroyed Jerusalem. Someone else will carry out this destruction on our behalf and be happy ("happy is he...") about ridding the world of the evil.

Saddam Hussein told us himself that the war was really between him and the Jews. Everyone thought this was only a ruse to break up the coalition, but our rabbis teach us differently. This is from the Zohar (the seminal book of Jewish mysticism), written at least 1,800 years *ago: "Rabbi Abba said in the name of Rabbi Yossi the Elder, and Rabbi Shimon also said, the Holy One will bring to life again to all the kings who afflicted Israel and Jerusalem: Hadrian, Lupinus, Nebuchadnezzar, Sancherib, and all the other kings who destroyed His Temple. He will set them up again as rulers, and they shall gather many nations, and then He will do vengeance and justice on them near Jerusalem, as it is written, 'And this will be the plague with which the Lord will smite all the peoples that have fought against Jerusalem.' (Zechariah 14:12)*[51]

The prophet Jeremiah, who himself followed the Jews into the Babylonian exile, consoled his people by prophesying that justice will be done to Babylon. Here's what he says: "Thus says the Lord—behold, I will arouse upon Babylon and upon the dwellers of the land of Kasdim a destroying wind. (A Desert Storm?) And I will send to Babylon spoilers, and they will spoil her and empty out her land, for they surround her. Against he that draws the bow will the bow be drawn, and against those that go up in armor; don't spare her young men, destroy the entire army. Thus corpses will fall in the land of Kasdim, and those that are pierced will fall in the streets.[52]

In Kuwait and southern Iraq, the scenes have been astonishing. The Allies destroyed Iraqi forces in a crushing land battle that General Schwartzkopf dubbed "The Hammer." Everyone marveled at the Allies' twenty-first century war technology. Video cameras were attached to the noses of laser-guided missiles so we could all see, first hand, the destruction of the entire Iraqi infrastructure. Even thick blankets of black smoke couldn't stop the onslaught of the "smart bombs." Reporters marveled as they watched convoys of trucks moving north on the highways with their headlights on at high noon. Only a small crack of light on the horizon gave proof that it was daytime.

At night, the fury of two hundred blazing oil fires lit up the midnight sky. The noxious vapors of the burning crude oil filled the air. Pollution experts say that the ecological devastation will be greater than that of the oil spill that covered the sea. The chemical residue in the air was the same as that from the tar in cigarettes and could have devastating consequences for the population for years to come. The onslaught was merciless. The sobbing cries of frightened Iraqi soldiers and commanders were picked up live from intercepted field radio broadcasts.

The devout Jew continued his account:

It is uncanny to read the ancient words of the prophets while watching these events unfold before our very eyes.

The Jewish prophets told us that not only would Babylon and Kasdim be destroyed, but also how it would be done and what the battle would look like. Here is how Isaiah described the future destruction of Iraq, *more than two thousand years ago. Don't forget that Nebuchadnezzar's regime was overthrown in an overnight, bloodless coup by the Persian empire. Since ancient times there has been no great destruction in that region. But now—*

Her (Babylon's) rivers will be turned to tar, her dust to brimstone, her land to burning tar. Night and day it won't be extinguished; her smoke will go up forever.[53]

Jeremiah predicts the future war this way: "For, lo, I will arouse and cause to come against Babylon a gathering of great nations from the land of the north, and they shall arrange themselves against her. From there she shall be taken; their arrows shall be like those of a death-dealing warrior. They won't return empty." Rabbi Meir Leibush, in his classical Biblical commentary describes these "death-dealing arrows" that never miss their targets as follows: The arrows of the enemy [i.e.,the enemy of Babylon] will seem as if they have intelligence and they come by themselves to their target. They won't return empty, like a smart warrior [doesn't return empty handed].[54]

Jeremiah further describes the events of the battle in Babylon and Kasdim: And Kasdim will be despoiled...The sound of war is in the land, and great destruction. How the hammer cuts off and breaks the whole land; how Babylon has become a desolation among the nations. I have laid a trap for you and also *have caught you, Babylon, and you did not know, you are found and also caught because you antagonized the Lord... Gather many together to Babylon, all those who know to shoot arrows, camp against her, encircle her, don't let any escape; pay her back according to her deeds. Like all that she did, do to her... Therefore her youth shall fall in the streets and all her men of war will be cut down on that day... And they will be like women [weak like women who don't fight against their enemies]*[55] *The king of Babylon has heard the report and his hands have become weak, the anguish causes him to tremble like a woman in labor... From the sound of the taking of Babylon, the land shudders and the cry is heard among the nations."*[56]

Even though I haven't been using a gas mask, we still take the whole family to the sealed room that we prepared. The prophet Isaiah tells us: "Go, my people, come into your rooms and shut your doors around you; hide for a short moment until the fury passes."[57]

The Psalmist adds that we will be safe indoors: "You will not be afraid of the fear at night, of the arrow that flies by day; of the plague that goes by day nor of the destruction that wastes at noon." Rabbi Meir Leibush, again, writing more than a hundred and twenty years ago, explains that "*the destruction that wastes at noon.*"[58] *means,* "Do not be afraid of poisonous air."[59]

PART IV

Miracles

From
Lucky
To
Miraculous

◀
◀
◀
◀
◀
◀
◀
◀
◀
◀
◀

February 3, 1991

When one person manages to escape from death, we say he was lucky.

When a few people are involved, we are amazed how they cheated fate.

When dozens, and even hundreds of people walk away from the devastating horror of a missile attack, they have defied all laws of chance and probability. That is what we call "miraculous."

This is how one man tells his story:

I was at home alone the night the missile fell. Right after the siren went off, I heard the phone ring. It was my friend David. I told him that I had this feeling something was going to happen. He laughed and told me only three minutes had gone by since the alarm was sounded and that I still had two minutes to get ready. I had this dreadful feeling inside. A minute and a half later there was an explosion. I didn't have a mask on *and my room wasn't really sealed properly. There were only a couple of sheets of plastic on the windows.*

Most of the house was destroyed. Luckily the room I was in was left standing. I wasn't injured at all, even though broken glass and pieces of plaster went flying past me. I was standing opposite a mirror and it shattered all around me. If I would have been in the center of the room, everything would have landed on me because the window and door were torn out of their frames and thrown against the opposite wall. When everything settled down, it was completely dark, and the telephone was cut off. When I turned on the emergency light near me, I could see the room was still standing, but everything in it was destroyed. Out of my whole bar, only a couple of bottles were left in one piece. I came back the next day with some friends to show them what I had walked away from and we opened one of the remaining bottles and raised a cup "to life," LeChayim![60]

Another survivor related this story:

When the siren sounded at about 2:00 A.M., Meir and his brothers—neighbors of mine from the building next door—came to me and asked me not to stay at home alone. I guess they figured an old lady like me couldn't take care of herself in the middle of the night. They asked me to return with them to their house to wait out the attack. They said they wanted me to feel more secure. I agreed. A few seconds later, just after we left my house, but before we reached theirs, the missile fell right in the alley between my house and theirs, totally destroying both houses![61]

A fateful choice saved hundreds:

It was a miracle from heaven. Fully as great as the extent of the damage is the extent of the miracle. When the missile crashed into the public shelter in the courtyard, hundreds of people were sitting in an adjoining shelter, only meters away. It's simply unbelievable. We suggested that they go into this shelter over here, which was destroyed by the missile, but for some reason they preferred to go into the other one, and were saved. I don't even want to think about what would have happened if the missile had fallen just two hundred meters away from here on the residential buildings.[62]

*Inspecting the remains of the thankfully
unoccupied shelter.*

Many have been lucky enough to be at the right place at the right time.

Shimon and Reena were two of the lucky ones:

The siren woke us out of our sleep. We got out of bed and hurried to the sealed room. Moments after we left the bedroom, we heard the blast. The house shook and the lights went out.

We lit some candles to inspect the damage. The sealed room that we were in was almost totally untouched. The windows that were covered with sheets of plastic broke, but they didn't shatter into the room. The ceiling caved in slightly, but the pictures were still hanging on the walls. My husband and I didn't have a scratch on us.

It wasn't until we began wandering through the house with our candles that we realized how lucky we were. In the kitchen, the windows and shutters lay *shattered. There were holes in the ceiling and roof tiles had fallen into the living room. In our bedroom, the whole ceiling had collapsed onto our bed. If we would have been a little slower to react to the siren, we would have been crushed.*

I don't know if they'll be able to fix the house or if they'll have to tear it down. But it's really not important; it's only wood and stone. What is important is that we're alive and in one piece.[63]

Some people decided their best protection was the sealed room.

T*hirty missiles had already landed, all with regular warheads. There was a lot of discussion in the neighborhood on whether to go down to the bomb shelters or to the sealed room, so when the siren went off this time I had a hard time deciding what to do. In the end I ran to the sealed room and sat down on a chair just in time to hear the tremendous boom!*

I flew up almost to the ceiling and fell back to the floor. I knew right away that my house was gone. The bed that I was sleeping in a few minutes before was totally destroyed, and large pieces of glass were lodged in it. I thought I must have been the only person left alive in the neighborhood, it was so quiet outside. I didn't have the courage to go outside until I heard voices. I was crying and I yelled out, "I'm in here, I'm in here!" They came to take me out. I can't imagine what would have happened if I'd been caught on the way to the shelter.[64]

This is how others described their experiences:

The siren woke me up at about 1:30 in the morning. I live alone in an old house. I went to my sealed room and sat down on the floor. I don't remember hearing anything. Not the sound of the incoming missile or the Patriots. I don't even remember hearing the explosion.

The next thing I knew, the whole house had collapsed down around me. I was trapped by the debris. Only my head from the neck up wasn't buried. The rest of my body was stuck between broken concrete and metal.

When I opened my eyes, everything was dark and quiet. I checked to make sure I could feel all the parts of my *body. My arms were trapped and I couldn't remove my gas mask.*

About twenty minutes later the rescue crews arrived and sealed off the area. They carefully started moving away debris with their hands in order to cut a path toward me. They were all worried that any wrong move would cause everything to collapse on top of me. At the hospital, the doctors told me I only suffered minor cuts and bruises, and a large scratch on my back.[65]

Others decided the bomb shelter would be a better bet.

We decided to go down to the bomb shelter rather than to the sealed room when we heard the siren. After a few minutes, we heard a tremendous explosion, and all the windows in the house shattered. My mother jokingly said that the rescue workers would probably be looking for us. It sounded to us like only some windows had broken.

When we got upstairs though, we realized it was no joke. There wasn't a window left in the house. Some of them had been torn away with their frames. Everything was broken open. The front door had blown out. The dogs were gone, and we looked everywhere for them. About two hours later they came back. It was luck that they had been outside, and that we had been in the *shelter. Who knows what would have happened if we would have all been in the sealed room at the time?*[66]

Some weren't so smart. They made the wrong decision, but still managed to survive.

O*n Thursday, I had an argument with my daughter who lives in Tel Aviv. I wanted her to come spend the weekend with me. I said to her, "Our neighborhood's already been hit—it can't happen again. Now it's more dangerous where you live." She argued the exact opposite: "If Saddam hit a bull's eye once, he'd aim again at the same spot." In the end I won out, and she agreed to come with her husband and six-month-old son.*

When the alarm sounded, we ran to the sealed room and put on our gas masks. We expected to hear that the missile fell in the territories like the previous attack. Suddenly we felt two loud booms, and then a third blast, that was the strongest of all. The whole house shook, and everything around us collapsed. Doors were blown from their hinges, windows went flying, plaster rained down from the ceiling and everything went black.

After a few minutes we started looking for each other. In the dark, I yelled everybody's name. They all answered except for my daughter. I panicked, but eventually I found her, collapsed beside a table that had fallen on its side. I slapped her a few times and she woke up.

As she was coming to, she asked about the baby. I realized that in the confusion we'd totally forgotten to look for him. Frantically I started turning over every block of concrete. With each block, I said to myself, "just let me not find him here, because if he's under this, he's totally crushed. God, don't do this to me." My daughter started crying and pulling her hair. She screamed at me, "It's your fault if he's dead—it's all your fault! I'll hate you for the rest of my life. You're a murderer—you made us come here!"

My whole body started shaking. Nobody else was moving except me, searching through the rubble like a maniac. In the end, I saw the edge of the plastic tent peeking out from another corner of the room. The baby was lying in the tent with his eyes closed. My heart started pounding until I touched him and saw that he was breathing. My daughter eventually calmed down, but I still haven't been able to forgive her.[67]

This family couldn't make a decision whether
to stay in Tel Aviv or go to Jerusalem.
They compromised—and still were saved.

We arrived from the Soviet Union ten months ago. We were lucky we found an apartment to rent in Ramat Gan. When the war broke out, my wife was very nervous about staying in Tel Aviv. I have nerves of steel and wanted to stay. We discussed it a lot, *and finally, one morning she left with our two children to wait out the war in Jerusalem. I stayed in the apartment. She had a feeling something was going to happen that night.*

I was home alone when the siren went off. Suddenly, the power went out. I jumped past the cupboard toward the sofa. The missile landed only a few yards from our building, and the blast blew the window into the room. I crawled under the sofa, and all the walls fell down on top of me. A lot of concrete fell onto the sofa—that's what saved me. The balconies fell to the ground and the kitchen was totally destroyed. I was glad my wife and children had left. If they would have been at home, we all probably would have been in our little sealed room at the time. A terrible tragedy would have occurred. When the apartment is fixed, we hope to move back in. There is a saying in the Russian army: "No bomb or missile ever falls in the same place twice."[68]

Another family changed its mind twice in one day.
Their indecision saved their lives.

Two *days before the attack, my sister in Herzalia invited us to stay with her. We packed up some suitcases, loaded the three kids into the car, and off we went. My husband wasn't comfortable with all of us staying together in one house and insisted we return to our own apartment in Ramat Gan.*

When we got back, my brother-in-law phoned again. He was worried that our neighborhood wasn't safe. He really pressured us, and so we loaded up the car again, and back we went to my sister's place. That's how it came to be that we weren't in our apartment when the missile hit. It was a miracle.

When we returned to inspect the damage, we discovered that our building was completely demolished. There wasn't one thing left intact from our two-bedroom apartment except for pieces of the missile. The refrigerator was folded up like a rag. The computer was melted out of shape. Now, on the first of the month, the bank will be deducting our regular mortgage payment to pay for nothing.[69]

All that remained
of homes full
of memories,
was rubble.

Even The Believers Can't Believe It

◄◄◄◄◄◄◄◄◄◄◄◄◄

February 10, 1991

Many residents in neighborhoods struck by Scuds are religious Jews.

Their confidence that they will be protected in the Holy Land is almost beyond belief—and then it happens ...

Here is how Rachel sees it:

I'm sure that the miracle that happened in our neighborhood was partially the result of a special prayer service we had in the community synagogue earlier that day. We held a day of prayer and fasting. We recited Psalms and circled the synagogue carrying the Torah scrolls and blowing the shofar (ram's horn) in order to annul any difficult heavenly decree against the people of Israel. The atmosphere was just like Yom Kippur.

After we returned home and ended our fast, I sat down on the bed to do some knitting. To my surprise the siren was sounded, and we ran into our sealed room. The terrifying explosion above our heads threw the whole neighborhood into darkness. To my right, a huge hole was blown open in the wall that revealed the street below. We smelled a strong odor of gas; a propane tank below began leaking. As luck would have it, the water pipes also ruptured and extinguished a small fire that would have caused the propane tank to explode. All ways out were sealed by blocks of concrete and rubble. The door wouldn't open and we had no idea how to save ourselves. In the end I squeezed out of a hole that had broken open in the living room wall. I called out for help.

There was no answer. I was terrified. I was sure we must have been the only ones to have survived because there was a strange quietness during those first few moments. Also, from the scene of devastation in front of us, we concluded that everyone—God forbid—was lost. But just then—people began to stream out from between the fallen buildings, and to our amazement we realized that everyone was alive! Because of the terrible shock, no one could open their mouths during the first few moments. With every neighbor appearing healthy and in one piece (except for minor scratches and wounds from flying bits of plaster and broken glass), our joy increased. We know that because of the merit of the prayers and the Psalms that we recited earlier that day, *with our tears and heartfelt intentions, that the whole neighborhood was saved in body and spirit.*[70]

"From the scene of devastation in front of us, we concluded that everyone was lost ..."

There is an old saying, "Throughout history, more than the Jews kept and protected the Sabbath, the Sabbath kept and protected the Jews." For many Israeli families, this proved to be true.

There were nine of us in the house at the time; my husband and I, our three single children, our son and his wife, and a cousin from Jerusalem and his wife. Everyone had come to spend the Sabbath together.

When the siren went off, we all crowded into the sealed room. It was really too small to hold all of us comfortably. The two wives were both in their last months of pregnancy. Each tried to convince the other to sit down in the only armchair in the room. While they were both standing up arguing, we heard the tremendous explosion. Suddenly, something smashed through the ceiling and part of it fell on my husband Yossi's knee, breaking it. When the dust cleared we could see what had come through the ceiling. A large piece of the missile was sitting on what used to be the armchair.[71]

Another family, ironically of Iraqi origin, had another Sabbath story to tell:

We *are a fairly traditional Jewish family from Baghdad. On Friday nights I light the candles and my husband recites the Kiddush blessing over the wine. Just after we finished Kiddush this particular Friday night, the siren went off. We managed to get into our sealed room along with our visiting nine-year-old granddaughter. Suddenly, the door was torn from its place and flew through the air, landing on the backs of our necks like a wall, shielding us. Then came the terrible blast from the shock wave and the window shattered with tremendous force into the room. It sprayed splinters of glass onto everything. After the noise quieted down, we were shocked by the power of the blast. Pieces of glass were stuck into the wall an inch deep. The* *door was filled with holes. Pictures on the walls were punctured. If the door wouldn't have uprooted itself and landed on the angle that it did on our necks, we would have been seriously injured by the hailstorm of glass. We saw the hand of God—He protected us and in His mercy we were saved.*[72]

The force of the blasts sent shattered glass flying in every direction.

Whole apartments were destroyed—but holy books
and ritual objects remained intact.

This is one family's story:

I was unemployed for the past month. Out of
desperation I went to see a famous rabbi in Bnei
Brak for advice. He gave me a blessing for success and
promised that I would find a job to support my family.
But he required me to keep the Sabbath and to not shave
my beard. As I said, I was desperate, so I accepted his
conditions. At the same time, my wife became more
interested in Judaism and decided to have a local rabbi
check the mezzuzot (ritual parchments containing hand-
written biblical verses) on the doors of our apartment.
The rabbi determined that the mezzuzot had been
damaged and that they had to be replaced with new
ones. Even though our financial situation was desperate,
we somehow found the money to pay for the expensive
parchments.

A couple of days later, a Scud missile hit one meter
from our building. Everything in the apartment was
uprooted from its place. Our gas masks flew right off of
our faces and the shock wave sent the shoes flying off our
feet. Cupboards, windows, toys—everything was
destroyed. The door frames were uprooted with
tremendous force, and the doors as well. Only the
mezzuzot remained firmly attached to the door frames.
"The vessel broke and we escaped." Our house was
destroyed, yet we and our children walked away.[73]

Another family related this:

The day after the explosion, we returned to our destroyed apartment to see if anything was left. In the place where our home had been there was only a pile of sand, stones and shattered walls. Nothing seemed to be left. Only after some minutes did we identify one object that had survived intact, sitting in the rubble: It was the bag containing my husband's tallis and tefillin [prayer shawl and phylacteries], and a prayer book for the Yom Kippur services.[74]

Incredible accounts like this one
are becoming almost daily occurrences:

When the missile hit, we couldn't make it to the sealed room. That room was completely destroyed. If we would have been in the sealed room, we would have been riddled with holes from the flying glass that hit everything in sight. We've been telling reporters all day that we were saved by an open miracle, by the hand of Divine Providence, but it seems that they're hesitant about emphasizing the miraculous aspect that we so strongly feel. I was unhurt, but my watch is no longer working. Look, it stopped when it was hit by a piece of shrapnel—it's stuck at 6:05, the exact moment of the blast.

The bookcase stood here. After a piece of the missile ripped through the wall, the debris and the shock wave destroyed everything. All the books went flying along with the bookcase. Only the top shelf remained standing on the supports. That's where I keep my Bible and Talmud. Not one of those holy books fell to the ground, even though they were closer to the place where the missile fell.

A lot of reporters came and photographed the bookcase when they heard the story about the holy books, but for some reason no one ever published it except for one religious magazine.[75]

Not all reporters were so uncooperative. Some in the press began having a hard time just reporting the facts. The facts were too unbelievable.

This is one example:

A *missile punches through a reinforced concrete air raid shelter empty of people, sparing residents huddling behind masking tape and plastic sheeting in their homes a few meters away. It is almost enough to turn atheists into agnostics.*[76]

The Lawyer's Reprieve

◄ **January 24, 1991**

The streets of Israel are quiet, but tense. People are scurrying home; not so much because of the missiles, but because it is Friday afternoon; the Sabbath is approaching.

In this mostly religious neighborhood, all the food is prepared, the tables are set with fine white linen, and people are wearing their best clothes to greet the Sabbath. David returns home early from his law office today. His wife lights the Sabbath candles, and he leaves for synagogue to attend Friday evening prayer services.

This is David's story:

The services ended at about 6:00 p.m. I stayed a little later than usual to study with a few friends. We left the synagogue together and while we were walking in the street, just before we reached my house, we heard the siren. My first thought was to run to my house, to be with my wife and children. But on second thought, because the people I was walking with were elderly, I decided to stay with them. They lived quite far from the synagogue and wouldn't be able to make it home in time.

We took shelter in the lobby of a nearby building. I didn't have my gas mask with me. We all started reciting Psalms from memory. I noticed two small children, maybe six or seven years old, who were caught outside with us. They were hugging each other, reciting "Shema Yisrael" (Hear O' Israel...) the traditional prayer Jews say when facing danger. While I was watching the children, I suddenly heard the bursts of the Patriots being fired. I knew the danger was nearby because the Patriots were fired from our neighborhood. The noise from the Patriots was frightening, and the two little children hugged each other even tighter.

Then I saw a big burst of fire from the exploding Scud hitting the ground. It was an enormous blast, and we all shook and shivered. We were only about one hundred and fifty yards from where it landed, and the force of it threw us backwards. Then we saw the dust and the fire rising from the ground, coming from the direction of my house. I remember yelling, "It's my house!"

I started running home. As I came nearer, I saw that it really was my house that was hit. From about fifty yards away, I couldn't see the house because of the black smoke and the fire and the water spraying out of the broken water pipes. Gas was leaking and power lines were down. At first I thought it was a chemical attack because of the smell of gas in the air. Right at that moment, I thought to myself, "I'm glad I didn't bring my mask." Who would want to live if something happened to his family? We'd already had a tragedy at home with one son, and I remember thinking to myself that I couldn't stand any more tragedy.

Next door to my house, I saw a three-story building had collapsed, as well as two smaller buildings even further away. I thought, my God, if they collapsed then nothing could be left of my house. I started shouting, but no one answered. I managed to get into the garden and went around the house to the place where I knew that my wife and children would have been sitting in our so-called "sealed room." We didn't have a bomb shelter in our house. If we did, they would have gone there. I couldn't reach the room because the bricks and walls of the three-story building had fallen toward my house. I couldn't tell if anything was left of the back of the house where they were sitting.

I remember climbing over a pile of bricks and shouting, but no answer came from inside. I was sure that no one was left. Later, after about fifteen minutes, I heard voices from the house. I saw my fifteen-year-old daughter step out with her puppy. Then my younger son came out, and finally my wife. When I saw them all alive, I told them, "Let's first of all say something to thank God—I don't believe that you are alive!"

My wife started crying. When she saw the damage and destruction to the neighbors' homes, she started screaming, "They're all killed, they're all killed!"

We went to the other houses. I helped an old woman who lived on the third floor in the next building. She started yelling at me, "I can't go down the stairs, I can't go down the stairs!" I told her that it was okay—that she was already on the ground. She told me her husband was still upstairs. I saw we couldn't take him out because there were all kinds of bricks on top of him. Later, I saw his picture on the television and that he was okay. He was only slightly wounded.

I went to the two other small houses that had collapsed. "Collapsed" isn't even a good word for it. The walls were gone. You couldn't even tell where the houses originally stood. I thought these neighbors must surely be dead. Later, slowly, slowly, it became clear that no one was killed. They were only slightly injured. Everyone had his own story of how he had survived. This one was going from one room to another; another was on the staircase; someone else was outside; this one went to make Kiddush at a friend's house. It was as if they weren't the masters of their own fates. It was as if they were riding on waves, being taken places.

From that moment I saw that we aren't in control of anything. It's as if we got a warning of sorts: God caused damage to our property—which is nothing, only material things—and not to our lives—which are more important. Later the soldiers and the police came and said, "We have to guard your houses and property because someone might steal something." I started to laugh. I told them, it's not important anymore.

A reporter from CNN asked me, "How do you explain this?" I told him that everything that happened to me that night was a miracle. If I hadn't insisted on staying in the synagogue to study after prayers, I would have come home fifteen minutes earlier. I would have gathered the family together to say the Kiddush over the wine in the dining room. I am sure, knowing myself, that I would have insisted that my family stay to finish the blessings even when the siren went off, and to not go to the sealed room. I have my own pride, and I wasn't going to let that man from Baghdad tell me when to do the Kiddush and when not to do the Kiddush. The place where we would have been standing was completely ruined. Who knows what would have happened?

And then, if I had decided to run home quickly when the siren went off, someone would have come to the door to let me in, instead of staying in the sealed room. Who knows what would have happened to the both of us, standing at the front door?

I don't know if it is right to say it, but I think that we are living in a time of miracles. I saw another miracle a week ago, on Saturday. At 2:30 in the morning another Scud hit, which was to my regret near my mother's house in another neighborhood. We were living with her at the time. My mother's house wasn't damaged too much—just some broken windows. But when we heard the bomb, I knew it was very, very near.

I ran out, and I think I was one of the first people to see the damage. It was something unbelievable. Tens, maybe hundreds of apartments were ruined. Half apartments, quarter apartments, balconies torn away, rooms torn away. I was watching this destruction at night just before 3:00 a.m., and I couldn't believe what I was seeing. I never saw such vast destruction like this in my life.

At that moment I remember saying to myself, "Oh God, I hope... I hope, I pray that today there won't be tens, or even hundreds killed." I was sure that this time our good luck, or protection, had been taken away from us. Just then a Civil Guard rescue worker asked me what I thought. He was also in shock from the scene in front of him. I told him, as I look around, I can't see the end of the destruction. I can't believe that we will go away from here without finding at least one hundred people dead.

I couldn't stand it anymore, and I went home. I was in such a bad mood because it was the second time I'd seen an attack, and I was afraid that this time someone wasn't protecting us anymore. In my eyes, all I could see was the destruction. And when I heard later, from the outside and on the radio, that only tens of people were slightly injured, I couldn't believe that there were any more miracles left to be shown to us. Because it was really unbelievable. You could not believe it if you didn't *see it. They said later in official announcements that five hundred apartments were damaged—but no one was killed.*

As I said before, there's not much we can do about it. The waves are guiding us to the shore. At least I hope it is the shore. We are only getting signals. Signals that may be telling us to do something, to change something. They are warnings, not punishments. The houses and apartments will be rebuilt. Jews will help us from abroad. You see people already wanting to help each other, and it makes you feel so warm that you don't need to put on clothes to keep you warm. In any place I go, if anyone hears about us or others, they all offer so much, from the municipality to friends and even people we don't know. People want us to come and stay with them or live with them. Here, look at this: I have a drawer full of keys that people have given to us to their apartments, telling us to come to their homes whenever we want, even if they aren't there.

I think such a thing can only happen in Israel. To see such miracles, and to see such reactions from people—because such a feeling, at such a time, is worth more than all the money in the world. I hope that the worst has passed. We are praying for peace.[77]

Epilogue: The End Is Just The Beginning

◄ *February* **28, 1991**

◄ The streets of Israel
◄ are filled with children
◄ and adults wearing
◄ masks.
◄ This time they are not
◄ gas masks, but the
◄ traditional costumes
◄ celebrating the Jewish
◄ festival of Purim.

People walk to synagogue, carrying their gas masks in boxes slung over their shoulders. It is the morning of February 28, 1991. Inside the synagogues, the Book of Esther is read aloud. It is the story of a great reversal of fortune for the Jewish people. The wicked viceroy of Persia, Haman, had plotted to murder all the Jews in the kingdom. Through a sequence of inexplicable and miraculous events, the tables were turned, and through the efforts of the Jewish leaders Mordechai and Queen Esther, Haman was hung on the very day that he had chosen to kill the Jews. For the last twenty-five hundred years, Purim has been a day of celebration of the triumph of good over evil.

This is what happened in our home this morning.

When I returned from synagogue that morning, my children greeted me with singing and laughing. While we had been reading about the destruction of Haman, George Bush had announced that the Allied forces called a cease fire. My six-year-old asked if they would write a book about Saddam Hussein that would be read in synagogue next year! I smiled. In her own way, she could sense the cycle of history repeating itself.

Later that morning, at 10:00 A.M., Brigadier General Nachman Shai announced that everyone could remove the plastic sheeting from their windows and put away their gas masks. The threat of Scud missiles was over. We could start getting back to normal.

I rushed to the bedroom and ripped the brown plastic tape off the door and window frames. And in my mind's eye, I again saw my family huddled together in our sealed room only a few days before. A thought occurred that gave me hope for the future. My daughter's comment about Saddam recalled our people's history of two thousand years of exile. We Jews have been scattered to the four corners of the earth. Wherever we were, we were plagued by persecution, pogroms and the Holocaust. Ironically, while all the enemies of the Jewish people eventually disappeared, the Jews themselves survived.

I recalled the "all clear" being sounded for the last time. The announcement was made in foreign languages for those Israelis who had not yet learned Hebrew. For five minutes, the room was filled with a stream of voices: French, English, Russian, Rumanian, Ethiopian; some of the languages Jews had learned during their long exile. That's when I realized I was witnessing the biggest miracle of all. The Jewish people were finally coming home.

NOTES

1. Jerusalem Report, February 21, 1991 (p. 17)
2. Mishpacha, Special War Edition, February 1991 (p. 24)
3. Mishpacha, Special War Edition, February 1991 (p. 27)
4. S. C., Jerusalem

PART I
5. M. M., Jerusalem
6. N. B., Jerusalem
7. A. K., Jerusalem
8. Yediot Achronot, January 27, 1991 (p. 1)
9. S. W., Ramat Gan
10. S. G., Jerusalem
11. Yediot Achronot, February 5, 1991 (p. 1)
12. Israel Government Press Office, based on Doron Brosh's commentary in Maariv, January 20, 1991 (Section 2, p.3)
13. Hadashot, January 21, 1991 (Amnon Dankner)
14. Jerusalem Post, January 21, 1991 (p. 5)
15. Jerusalem Post, January 21, 1991 (p. 5)
16. Interview L. K., Jerusalem
17. Jerusalem Post, February 25, 1991 (Herb Keinon, p.12)
18. Jerusalem Post, February 11, 1991 (Danny Sanderson, p. 5)

PART II
19. Mishpacha, Special War Edition, February 1991 (p. 31)
20. Mishpacha, Special War Edition, February 1991 (p. 24)
21. Hadashot, January 20, 1991
22. Jerusalem Post, February 12, 1991 (Bradley Burston, p. 1)
23. Yated Neeman, February 15, 1991 (p. 21)
24. Jerusalem Report, February 21, 1991 (p. 17)
25. S. J., Ramat Gan
26. L. R., Tel Aviv
27. Israel Government Press Office, February 28, 1991
28. Hadashot, February 5, 1991 (Michal Kedem, p. 19)

PART III
29. Hadashot, February S. 1991 (Ronit Weiss-Berkovich p. 21)
30. Jerusalem Report, February 21, 1991 (Sara Averick, p. 19)
31. Hadashot, February 10, 1991 (Michal Kedem, p. 5) Maariv, February 4, 1991
32. Jerusalem Post, February 1, 1991 (p. 3)
33. Mishpacha, Special War Edition, February 1991 (p. 27)
34. Hadashot, January 30, 1991 (Avi Small, p. 16)
35. Jerusalem Post, January 22, 1991 (p. 10)
36. Mishpacha, Special War Edition, (p. 31)
37. Jerusalem Post, January 21, 1991 (p. 10)
38. Jerusalem Post, January 27, 1991 (p. 8)
39. Jerusalem Post, February 8, 1991 (Walter Ruby, p. 1)
40. Hadashot, February 10, 1991 (Michal Kedem, p. 6)
41. Hadashot, January 20, 1991
42. Yediot Achronot, January 27, 1991 (p. 15)
43. Jerusalem Post, February 8, 1991 (Avigail Sturm, p. 11)
44. Jerusalem Post, February 8, 1991 (Avigail Sturm, p. 11)
45. C. K., Jerusalem
46. Hadashot, February 12, 1991 (Feldman, p. 2)
47. Yediot Achronot, January 20, 1991 (p. 15)
48. Yediot Achronot, January 20, 1991 (R. Shaked)
49. Jerusalem Post, January 24, 1991 (Abraham Rabinovich, p. 5)
50. Psalms 137:1
51. Zohar Beshalach 58b
52. Jeremiah 51:1-4
53. Isaiah 34:9-10
54. Malbim (Rabbi Meir Leibush) 1809 - 1879
55. Radak (Rabbi David Kimchi) 1157-1236 Narbonne, Provence
56. Jeremiah 50:10...46
57. Isaiah 26:20
58. Psalms 91
59. Malbim (Rabbi Meir Leibush) 1809 - 1879, commentary on Psalms 91

PART IV
60. Hadashot, February 13, 1991 (Ayal Ochna, p. 9)
61. Yediot Achronot, January 20, 1991
62. Al HaMishmar, January 20, 1991

63. Hadashot, February 13, 1991 (Ayal Ochna, p. 8)
64. Hadashot, February 10, 1991 (Michal Kedem, p. 5)
65. Personal interviews, and combined reports of Hadashot, Maariv and Yated Neeman (February 12 & 13, 1991)
66. Hadashot, February 12, 1991 (Feldman, p. 2)
67. Hadashot, February 10, 1991 (Michal Kedem, p. 5)
68. Hadashot, February 5, 1991 (Meir Turgeman, p. 18)
69. Hadashot, January 25, 1991 (Dorit Rishoni, p. 15)
70. Mishpacha, Special War Edition, February 1991 (p. 24)
71. Hadashot, February 10, 1991 (Gila Rosen, Meir Turgeman p. 4)
72. Mishpacha, Special War Edition, February 1991
73. Mishpacha, Special War Edition, February 1991 (p.24)
74. Combined Voice of Israel/Israel Army radio broadcast, January 20, 1991
75. Mishpacha, Special War Edition, February 1991
76. Jerusalem Post, January 25, 1991 (Abraham Rabinovich, p. 1)
77. D. K. Ramat Gan

LEVIATHAN PRESS
BOOKS THAT MAKE A DIFFERENCE

Newly Revised and Expanded
ROSH HASHANAH YOM KIPPUR SURVIVAL KIT
by Shimon Apisdorf
Bestselling recipient of a Benjamin
Franklin Award.

There you are; it's the middle of
High Holy Day services, and
frankly, you're confused. Enter—
the *Rosh Hashanah Yom Kippur
Survival Kit.* This book master-
fully blends wisdom, humor and
down-to-earth spirituality. It's like
having a knowledgeable friend
sitting right next to you in synagogue.

CHANUKAH
EIGHT NIGHTS OF LIGHT, EIGHT GIFTS FOR THE SOUL
by Shimon Apisdorf   1997 Benjamin Franklin Award

This book peels away the outer layers of Chanukah and
reveals a profoundly rich, spiritual core to the holiday.
Chanukah is about discovering the soul in the flame, the
soul in everyday life and the power of the soul in Jewish
history.

PASSOVER SURVIVAL KIT
by Shimon Apisdorf

This internationally acclaimed bestseller, serves as a friendly gateway through which you will enter the world of Passover and see it as you have never seen it before. The Passover Survival Kit enables you to experience one of the centerpieces of Jewish life as insightful, thought-provoking and relevant to issues of personal growth and the everyday challenges of life. This book stands on its own and also serves as a companion volume to *The Survival Kit Family Haggadah*.

THE SURVIVAL KIT FAMILY HAGGADAH
by Shimon Apisdorf

The only Haggadah in the world... **Featuring** the Matzahbrei Family. A loveable family of matzah people that guide you and your family through a delightful, insightful, spiritual and fun seder. **Featuring** the "talking Haggadah." A revolutionary translation. Never again will you read a paragraph in the Haggadah and say, "Huh, what's that supposed to mean?"

Written as a companion to the *Passover Survival Kit*.

REMEMBER MY SOUL
by Lori Palatnik

WHAT TO DO IN MEMORY OF A LOVED ONE
*Includes: A Guided Journey Through Shiva and
the Stages of Jewish Mourning*

*As a therapist and, as a mourner, I related to your book
in many ways. It helps one through the steps of
mourning and, to some degree, the acceptance of the
loss and incorporation of positive memories and lessons.*
Robbie Schwartz, Family Therapist

*Remember My Soul teaches the bereaved to harness the
rich resources of Jewish spirituality. It demonstrates
how to turn the pain of losing a dear one into a vehicle
for human wholeness.*
Rabbi E.B. Freedman, Director of Jewish Hospice
Services, Hospice of Michigan

THE BIBLE FOR THE CLUELESS BUT CURIOUS
FINALLY, A GUIDE TO JEWISH WISDOM FOR REAL PEOPLE
by Nachum Braverman

This book won't throw a bunch of "thous" and "forsooths" at you or or try to make you feel guilty. It *will* speak to you like the thoughtful human being that you are, and, by way of a gallery of icons, present the wisdom of the Bible in a fun and uniquely insightful fashion.

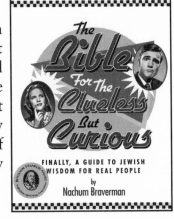

The Bible For The Clueless But Curious

FINALLY, A GUIDE TO JEWISH WISDOM FOR REAL PEOPLE
by
Nachum Braverman

About the Author

Charles Samuel is a former management consultant from Toronto, Canada. In 1983 he and his wife moved to Jerusalem. He speaks in Israel and abroad on a wide range of topics in Jewish thought and philosophy. Charles Samuel is the author of a best-selling Israeli novel, The Jerusalem Conspiracy and is currently working on his next book.

The author can be reached at
missiles@aish.edu